AWAY WE GO!

Away We Go!

*A guidebook of family trips
to places of interest in New Jersey,
nearby Pennsylvania, and New York*

Edited by MICHAELA M. MOLE

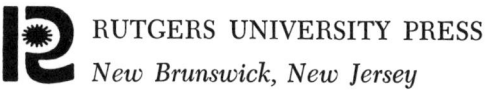

RUTGERS UNIVERSITY PRESS
New Brunswick, New Jersey

Third Revised Edition

ISBN: 0-8135-0694-8 Cloth Bound

0-8135-0696-4 Paper Bound

Copyright © 1961 by the JUNIOR LEAGUES OF NEW JERSEY

Copyright © 1963 by RUTGERS, THE STATE UNIVERSITY

Copyright © 1971 by RUTGERS UNIVERSITY, THE STATE UNIVERSITY OF NEW JERSEY

Library of Congress Catalogue Card Number: 63-23450

Manufactured in the United States of America by Quinn & Boden Company, Inc., Rahway, New Jersey

This book was originally a community service project of the eight Junior Leagues of New Jersey, under the supervision of Mrs. J. Wesley Albro.

The editor is grateful to individuals and organizations who furnished information and photographs for the present edition.

PREFACE

Although New Jersey received its name and became a British colony in 1664, its first European settlers, the Dutch, came much earlier—within ten years after the Pilgrims landed at Plymouth Rock.

From the beginning of our nation, New Jersey's history has been an impressive one. It was one of the first colonies to declare independence. Because of its position between New York and Philadelphia, Continental and British armies fought back and forth and Tory guerrillas harassed the civilian population. General Washington used the protecting hills of Morris County for encampments during three terrible winters when his army was without sufficient food, clothing, arms, or medical supplies, and central Jersey was the scene of some of Washington's greatest victories at Trenton, Princeton, and Monmouth. The seeds of the nation's navy were New Jersey coastal privateers who fought the mighty British blockade.

New Jerseyans were among the leaders of the fight against the pirates of the Barbary Coast in our war with Tripoli and then against the British in the War of 1812. When the Civil War broke out, New Jersey was among the first states to furnish volunteers.

Although cities have grown and suburbs have spread, much of New Jersey has remained for hundreds of years the beautiful land of the Lenni-Lenape Indians that Henry Hudson saw in 1609. Its mountains, lakes, rivers, and parks, and many miles of beaches have made New Jersey a joy to live in. Its rich soil has given New Jersey the name of "Garden State." As part of the largest port system in the world, its location makes it the roadway between North and South and a gateway to the West, with the highest diversity of industry in the nation.

Away We Go! is a guide through the past, present, and future of this area. There is so much to see, do, and enjoy in New Jersey that a whole year of exploring would hardly do it justice.

MICHAELA M. MOLE

East Brunswick, New Jersey
April, 1971

CONTENTS

HOW TO USE THIS BOOK

Away We Go! is a selection of hundreds of places to go and things to see in New Jersey as well as in New York City, Philadelphia, parts of Bucks County in Pennsylvania, and Orange and Rockland Counties in New York. All these places have been visited and evaluated by members of the Junior Leagues of New Jersey and all information has been rechecked for this edition. There may, however, be changes in rates and hours, and these should be checked in advance, particularly if a group tour or a trip to a far-off place is planned.

The map in the front of the book has been divided into areas along county lines which follow the chapters in the text. Within each section no place suggested for a trip is farther than fifty miles away. Therefore, for a round trip of one hundred miles or less in one day, pick out the section in which you live and refer to the matching place in the text. There are area maps before each chapter which are meant for orientation purposes only—detailed road maps are available at most gas stations. Each of the twenty-one counties in New Jersey publishes a detailed county map which may be obtained by writing to the Board of Chosen Freeholders at the county seat. Driving instructions, where necessary, are under the entries and begin at the nearest major highway or well-known city. Wherever the age level is important it is listed in the italicized information under the heading, as are times, rates, and other pertinent data.

When planning a group trip, it is well to remember that considerable notice is usually required at most plants and laboratories, and some historical sites and museums. Reservations should be made well in advance, giving the following information: number of adults and children, ages of the children or grades in school, and a choice of dates and hours for the visit.

SECTION 1

Sussex
Passaic
Morris
Bergen
Hudson
Essex

Our book starts with Sussex, northernmost county of New Jersey. It was settled in the early 1700's but as early as 1640 Dutch miners had explored the area in search of gold. Instead of gold these miners discovered copper deposits and one of the first commercial roads in the Colonies was built to transport it—the Old Mine Road that still runs through Warren and Sussex. Many of the earliest settlers of Sussex fought in the French and Indian War, providing a valuable nucleus of trained veterans for the Revolutionary forces. One of these was John Cleves Symmes; in 1774 he drew up a resolution for Sussex County, protesting taxation without representation. His committee joined with others to form the first Continental Congress. One of Symmes' daughters married William Henry Harrison, a President of the United States. The county's rich zinc deposits have been important to the nation's economy for over 140 years. For the visitor, however, Sussex is most important for its mountains and lakes.

Morris County began as an iron-mining settlement and its iron works were the arsenal for the Continental Army in the Revolution. One of the early Morris County iron magnates was Robert Erskine, a Scottish-born engineer who became Surveyor General of the Continental Army, and drafted the military maps used by Washington in the New Jersey campaign. His home, Ringwood Manor, is now a state park.

During two of the coldest winters of the war, Washington and his troops camped in Morristown. The general brought his army here in 1777 because the town provided a defensible position, near the iron works, against the British army stationed in New York. Washington stayed in Jacob Arnold's tavern while

1

his troops camped in the Loantaka Valley (site of the Loantaka Brook Reservation). In the winter of 1779 the general stayed at the Ford Mansion and his army was quartered in Jockey Hollow. Reconstructions and restorations of the encampment are in the Morristown National Historic Park.

Traces of the Morris Canal can still be found in both counties. One of the country's first canals, it was built without machinery; its purpose was to link Easton, Pennsylvania, with Newark (and later Jersey City). One of its guard locks has been preserved at Saxton Falls State Park where visitors can swim and fish.

Tending a lock on the Morris Canal near Stanhope. Date of picture unknown

Passaic, the "wasp-waisted" county, was settled in the late 1600's, becoming a county in 1837. Alexander Hamilton first saw the Totowa (Passaic) Falls while traveling with George Washington during the Revolution. He at once grasped its potential for industrial power and, in 1792, was a member of the charter group who built the nation's first cotton mill (in present-day Paterson).

Most of the Indians had been wiped out before 1647, the time when Manhattan Dutch established a trading post on the lands of Oratum, the sachem of the Hackensack Indians. This meant that the farmer settlers of Bergen County had a peaceful period to build up their holdings. This peace was destroyed during the Revolution when Bergenites suffered bitterly from the pillaging of British regulars and armed bands of Tories. One of the unhappiest incidents was the Baylor Massacre when an American detachment, sleeping in the Blauvelt House at River Vale, was slaughtered with bayonets by a British raiding party. By 1800, however, Bergen's rich soil had put its farmers back on their feet and they began to produce awesomely proportioned vegetables: notably, one-pound pears, three-foot celery and hundred-pound pumpkins. The county today is almost wholly residential and provides visitors with scenic drives and an interstate system of parks and historic sites along the Hudson River, connecting the county with neighboring New York State.

Dutch trappers had penetrated the wilderness of Hudson County as early as 1618. This was the land the Indians called "Hobocan-Hackingh"—land of the tobacco pipe. The first recorded land transfer in the state was made in 1629 when Michael Pauw obtained the grant for what is now Jersey City. For undetermined reasons he named the area Pavonia, "Land of the Peacock." Hoboken was the site of the country's first brewery (in 1642) and was incorporated by Colonel John Stevens, founder of the engineering family. Stevens built the first steam ferry; his son founded Stevens Institute of Technology, one of the world's great engineering schools. Jersey City (called Paulus Hook originally) occupies a peninsula between the Hudson and Hackensack rivers and it was here that the British occupied a fort during their occupation of New York. In Weehawkin, Alexander Hamilton was killed in his duel with Aaron Burr.

The world's first baseball game, between the Knickerbocker Giants and New York, was played in Hudson in 1846. The county's famous beer gardens made it the playground for New Yorkers before the Civil War. Its residents kept the underground railroad open between Hoboken and Jersey City.

Robert Treat and a group of settlers bought what is now Essex County from the Indians in 1665. A few years later they laid out the little village of Newark around Broad and Market Streets, with each settler receiving a six-acre plot. Initially, conditions were so rugged that bounties were paid for bears and wolves killed within the village. Dr. Aaron Burr, a Newark resident and father of the Vice-President, became the second president of the College of New Jersey (now Princeton). Essex is now one of the nation's most populous counties. Newark has gracious churches, lovely parks, and an excellent museum and library to draw visitors.

Reconstructed log hospital in Jockey Hollow Section, Morristown
National Historic Park

SPACE FARMS: ZOOLOGICAL PARK AND EARLY AMERICAN MUSEUM

Beemerville Road, Sussex, N.J. 07461 Tel.: (201) 875-5800

Hours: 9–7; open daily, April 15–Nov. 1. Fee: adults, $1.50; children, 50¢. Group fees: adults, $1.00; children, 50¢; no charge for teachers. Tours: by reservation only. Write for details.

Zoo with large collection of North American wild animals, birds, reptiles, 100 different species; also, animals and birds from other parts of the world. Early American and Indian Museum. Snake lecture with live snakes given to groups. Farm breeds minks; pens may be viewed; excellent small fur shop. Milking Parlor: demonstration of milking, 3:30 P.M. Restaurant; gift shop; picnic area and playground. Highly recommended for all ages. 1 entrance: no child may exit without adult. Summer antique car display.

On Rte. 519 in Beemerville, 6 miles west of Sussex. Follow signs.

Space Farms Leopard. *Leonard L. Rue III*

HIGH POINT STATE PARK

Sussex, N.J. Tel.: (201) 875-4800

Hours: daily, May 30–Labor Day; Sat., Sun., May 1–30 and and Labor Day–Oct. 31. Fees: Entrance, 25¢; children under 12, free; Parking, 50¢; High Point Monument, 25¢; motorless boats, $1.00.

In highest area in the state, park provides bathing, boating, fishing, hiking, picnicking, camping; High Point Monument may be climbed. Lodge with sleeping accommodations, restaurant.

On Rte. 23, 8 miles northwest of Sussex.

WAWAYANDA STATE PARK

P.O. Box 198, Highland Lakes, N.J. 07422

Located in Sussex County, this large mountain woodland tract is undeveloped but excellent fishing is available in the lake. Rowboats for rent; facilities for bathing, picnicking.

11 miles northeast of Hamburg, east of Rte. 94.

STOKES STATE FOREST AND STONY LAKE

R.D. Branchville, N.J. 07826   Tel.: (201) 948-3820

Hours: daily, May 30–Labor Day; Sat., Sun., May 1–30 and Labor Day–October 31. Fees: Entrance, 25¢ per person; children under 12, free; Parking, 50¢; campsite fees vary: check in advance.

Located on Kittatinny Ridge. Fine mountain country with outstanding scenery. Cabin and trailer sites available at Lake Ocquittunk. Bathing, boating, fishing, hunting, hiking. Picnic areas.

3 miles northwest of Branchville and 10 miles south of Milford, Pa., on Rte. 206.

SUSSEX COUNTY HISTORICAL SOCIETY

82 Main Street, Newton, N.J. 07860   Tel.: (201) 383-6010

Hours: Monday–Friday 9 A.M.–noon. Other times by appointment. No admission charge.

Permanent display of Indian artifacts, local material and an excellent genealogical library.

SWARTSWOOD STATE PARK

R.D. 2, Newton, N.J. 07860   Tel.: (201) 383-5320

Hours: daily, May 30–Labor Day; Sat., Sun., May 1–30 and Labor Day–October 31. Fees: Entrance, 25¢, children under 12, free; parking fee, 50¢; bathhouse, 25¢; rowboat rental, 75¢; motorless boats, $1.00.

Most of the state park on Swartswood Lake, noted for fishing; also, bathing, boating and picnicking at Emmons Grove.

4 miles north of Newton.

BUDD LAKE

Budd Lake, N.J. Tel.: (201) 347-9713

Open: Memorial Day–Labor Day. Fee: small fee for swimming; fee for boat rentals.

Natural lake with good fishing. Boat livery. Two public beaches. Picnic area and snack stand.

BERTRAND ISLAND AMUSEMENT PARK

Mt. Arlington, Lake Hopatcong, N.J. 07849 Tel.: (201) 398-0136

Hours: 11–11. Open Memorial Day–Labor Day. Admission free. Fees: for parking, amusements, swimming; group rates.

Rides and games on Boardwalk. Picnic area, restaurant.

2 miles off Rte. 46. Follow signs.

HOPATCONG BEAR FARM AND ZOO

Lake Hopatcong, N.J. 07849

Hours: Apr.–Nov. 1 (weather permitting), 10–dark. Fee: adults, 90¢; children, 50¢.

On west shore of Lake Hopatcong; entrance fee includes outdoor wild life movies. 150 live wild animals and birds.

Budd Lake

HOPATCONG STATE PARK

Landing, N.J. 07850

Hours: daily. Admission free.

On southwest shore of Lake Hopatcong (largest lake in New Jersey). Large picnic area; lake bathing; playground; snack stand; sightseeing boats. Boat rentals for pleasure and fishing at nearby state-owned public dock in Landing.

From exits of Routes 46, 206, and 80, follow signs to park.

Lake Hopatcong Historical Museum

Hopatcong State Park. Tel.: (201) 398-0248

Hours: open all year, Wednesdays only, 1–5; open at other times for groups or individuals by appointment: write Lake Hopatcong Historical Society, Box 36, Lake Hopatcong, N.J. 07849.

Six-room building, erected circa 1826, was home and office for Morris Canal gatekeeper. Now a museum, overlooking site of Morris Canal lock, feeder canal, and only known Scotch turbine in existence.

ROCKAWAY BOROUGH FREE LIBRARY

82 East Main Street, Rockaway, N.J. 07866   Tel.: (201) 627-5709

Hours: daily. Admission free.

Building is considered one of finest examples of its type between Morristown and Newton; built in early 1800's by Col. Jesse Jackson, early iron mining operator. Notable for the customary low kitchen, parlor, and enclosed staircase of the era.

Rte. 80, exit to Rockaway via Hibernia Road and Church St., and Rte. 46 via East Main St.

PICATINNY ARSENAL

Dover, N.J. 07801   Tel.: (201) 328-2102

Hours: open only upon written request. Tour: for organized groups, schools, by arrangement. Museum open to public, Fri., 9–3. Admission free.

The Arsenal, an agency of the U.S. Army Munitions Command, is involved in research and engineering for munitions.

On Rte. 15, one mile north of Dover.

GINGERBREAD CASTLE

Hamburg, N.J. 07419 Tel.: (201) 827-9540

Hours: daily from 10, Apr.–Oct. Weekends only, Nov.–Mar., 11–4. Fee: adults, 50¢; children, under 12, 35¢; children under 2, free.

Castle contains representations of fairy-tale characters, mostly from the Grimm brothers' German folk tales. Conducted tours led by expertly trained school children, dressed as Hansel and Gretel. Coffee shop.

MORRIS MUSEUM OF ARTS AND SCIENCES

Normandy Hgts. and Columbia Rd., Morristown, N.J. 07960 Tel.: (201) 538-0454

Hours: Mon.–Sat., 10–5, Sun. 2–5; closed major holidays. Summer (July through Labor Day): Tues.–Sat., 10–4; closed Sundays and Mondays. Admission and parking free. Group tours by prearrangement.

Exhibitions on electricity; sound; magnetism; space; live reptiles; mounted birds and mammals; North American Indians; model railroads; rocks and minerals; shells and fossils; foreign dolls. Collection of historic dolls and toys. Art, history, and other countries featured in changing exhibits.

From Morristown center to Columbia Road, left onto Normandy Heights Road.

BLACK RIVER PARK

Hacklebarney Rd., Chester, N.J.

County park with picnic sites; hiking; ice skating. Restored mill. Parking area.

On Rte. 24, 3 miles beyond Chester. Turn left on Hacklebarney Rd.

HACKLEBARNEY STATE PARK

Long Valley, N.J. 07853 Tel.: (201) 879-5677

Fees: for picnic tables.

In Morris County, this state park is beautifully situated in a gorge along the Black River. Facilities include picnicking, playground, hiking. Fishing in Black River and tributaries. Refreshment stand.

From Rte. 206, follow signs; between Somerville and Chester.

FLANDERS VALLEY GOLF COURSE

Rte. 206, Flanders, N.J. Tel.: (201) 285-6166 (County Park Commission)

Hours: daily. Fees: vary with time, age, group, county residency, etc.

27 holes; championship caliber. Pro shop; equipment rental; individual instruction. Winter: skating, skiing, sledding during daylight hours; no special equipment, tows, etc.

Northwest of Chester on Rte. 206; follow signs.

SILAS CONDICT PARK

Kinnelon Township, N.J.

Main feature of park is lake. Boat rentals (skeeter, rowboats); skating. Picnicking.

Off Rte. 23, west of Butler.

THE APPALACHIAN TRAIL

Trail for foot travel only, extends 2,000 miles from Maine to Georgia. In New Jersey it runs through High Point State Park and Stokes Forest to the Delaware Water Gap. U.S. 206, State Rte. 23, and several local roads that cross the Trail are marked with Trail symbol. One may take an hour's walk or a full day's hike, leaving car parked at entrance. Hikers should be careful not to leave behind rubbish that would deface the Trail for others. For extended hiking, Guidebook can be obtained from Appalachian Trail Conference, 1916 Sunderland Pl., NW, Washington, D.C. 20036.

FAIRY TALE FOREST

Oak Ridge, N.J. 07438 Tel.: (201) 697-5656

Hours: weekends, Easter Sunday to school closing; daily, from school closing to Labor Day; Winter: weekends from Labor Day to Thanksgiving.

Outdoor displays illustrating children's stories; miniature Swiss Village. Milk bar, lunchroom, restaurant. Particularly for small children. Amusement rides.

Rte. 513 to Rte. 231 west. Follow signs.

VERNON VALLEY SKI AREA

Route 94, Vernon, N.J. 07462 Tel.: (201) 827-6111

Hours: daily, 9:30–10:45; weekends, holidays, 8:30–10:45. Fees: vary for daylight, dusk, evening, etc.

Snow-making equipment. 4 lifts; 1 tow; 8 trails, novice through expert; vertical drop of 980 feet. Rentals and equipment sales; ski school, clinic. Cafeteria, cocktail lounge. No overnight lodging. Nursery; beginner-novice trail from top of mountain.

On Rte. 94, 1 mile west of Vernon.

GREAT GORGE SKI AREA, INC.

Box 848, McAfee, N.J. 07428 Tel.: (201) 827-9146

Hours: daily, 9:30–10:45. Fees: vary.

Snow-making equipment. Lifts; tows; 17 ski trails; 1 racing trail; vertical drop of 1033 feet. Rentals, sales of equipment. Ski school; clinic. Several eating facilities, no overnight lodging. No nursery but Toddler Ski School. Live entertainment, weekends.

Rtes. 94 and 517 at McAfee.

CRAIGMEUR SKI AREA

Green Pond Rd., Newfoundland, N.J. 07435 Tel.: (201) 697-4501

Hours: daily and evenings, Dec.–Mar. Fees: vary according to time, days.

Learners area; 3 open slopes; 2 trails; 1 T-Bar, 1 rope tow. Ski school. Equipment rental. Snack bar, restaurant, cocktail lounge.

From Rtes. 46 & 23 Circle: 16 miles north on Rte. 23 to Green Pond exit. Follow signs; about 2 miles.

SNOW BOWL SKI AREA

Weldon Rd., P.O. Oak Ridge, N.J. 07438 Tel.: (201) 697-6006

Hours: daily, 9–10:30; weekends, holidays, 8:30–10:30. Rates: vary for daylight, evening hours, etc. Call (201) 697-6024.

Snow-making equipment. Lifts; tows; 7 trails; 4 open slopes; vertical drop of 600 feet. Rentals; ski school; ski clinic. Tavern and lodge (no overnight lodging). Nursery. Lighted night skiing. Ice skating day and night. Outdoor heated pool open all year.

Off Rte. 23 at Oak Ridge Road. Follow signs.

LOANTAKA BROOK RESERVATION

Seaton-Hackney Farm

South St., Morristown, N.J. 07960   Tel.: (201) 539-3959

Hours: daily. Fee: charge for instruction, horses.

County Park system farm features individual and group riding lessons. Some horses for hire without instruction. Bridle paths; horse shows.

From Morristown center: south on South St.; one mile; stable on left.

Loantaka Pond

Kitchell Rd., Morris Township, N.J.

Admission free.

County park system with open areas for games; softball fields; fishing; coasting; ice skating (with big, warm fire) when flag is up.

From Morristown center; Rte. 24 (Madison Ave.) to Convent Station: turn onto Kitchell Road.

MORRIS COUNTY CENTRAL STEAM RAILROAD

Route 10, Whippany, N.J. 07981

Hours: April–Nov., Sat., Sun. and holidays, 1:30, 3, 4:30. Closed Thanksgiving Day. Fees: adults, $1.50; children, 75¢; special group rates.

Steam engine ride along old Whippanong Indian Trail, follows path taken by Washington's army in winter of 1779. Has one of oldest steam locomotives still in operation (1907); open flat car for camera fans; little red caboose for children; picnic grove, souvenir shop, snack stand.

On Rte. 10: westbound, use Whippany Road jughandle; eastbound, use Troy Road jughandle.

GREAT SWAMP OUTDOOR EDUCATION CENTER

Chatham Township, N.J. 07928   Tel.: (201) 635-6629

Hours: open daily. Admission free. Tours: weekdays for school groups only; weekend tours for adults; self-guided tours daily.

Guided tours over boardwalk path through this famous nature preserve; lectures on flora, fauna, etc. Arrangements can be made for "Nature Walks" through different county parks: guided tours with instructive talks.

Off Southern Blvd. in Chatham; follow signs.

MORRISTOWN NATIONAL HISTORIC PARK

The state's only national park commemorates the encampment of Washington and the Continental Army during the winter of 1779–80. Its separate areas are described below. For an ideal day's outing for the entire family start at the Ford Mansion, then to Jockey Hollow for a picnic lunch, then Wick House, with a side trip to Fort Nonsense if time permits. Other lunch facilities in Morristown center.

Statue of Patriot, Morristown National Park

Ford Mansion and the Historical Museum

230 Morris Ave. (Park headquarters), Morristown, N.J. 07960
Tel.: (201) 539-2016

Hours: daily, 10–5; closed Thanksgiving, Christmas and New Year's Days. Fees: adults, 50¢; children under 16, free when accompanied by adult. Tour: for school groups, 1½ hours; arrange in advance.

The Ford Mansion, or "Washington's Headquarters," built about 1772; restored, furnished with period pieces. Historical Museum contains collections of Revolutionary art, guns, household items, costumes; houses the original Gilbert Stuart portrait of Washington.

From Morristown center; north on Morris Ave.

13

Jockey Hollow Section

Jockey Hollow Section

Hours: daily until dark; closed Thanksgiving, Christmas and New Year's Days. Admission free.

Over 900 wooded acres, site of main Continental Army encampment, with reconstructed soldiers' and officers' huts; hospital. Park contains miles of nature trails; marked wildflower trail; wildlife sanctuary; picnicking but no fires permitted.

From Morristown center, right on Washington St.; north 2 blocks; left on Western Ave. Parking area about 3 miles farther on.

Fort Nonsense

Site of fort built 1777 by Washington's order for defense of hill.

From Morristown center; right on Washington St.; left on Western Ave.; first left. Follow signs.

14

Wick House and Farm

Hours: daily, 1–5; closed December and January and Thanks-giving Day. Admission free.

Restored and furnished farm house; military headquarters during encampment. Old-fashioned herb garden.

From parking area on Western Ave., west to Tempe Wick Rd. Turn right.

Tempe Wick House

LEWIS MORRIS PARK

Mendham Rd., Morristown, N.J. 07960   Tel.: (201) 285-6166

Hours: daylight. Admission free. Reservations required for large picnic groups (over 25); overnight camping for groups by per-mit.

Large county park; picnic sites; nature trails; camping; softball; skiing, coasting during daylight hours only. No skiing facilities.

On Rte. 24, 3 miles west of Morristown.

MACCULLOCH HALL MUSEUM

45 Macculloch Ave., Morristown, N.J. 07960   Tel.: (201) 538-2404

Hours: Mon.–Fri., 2–4, telephone in advance. Admission free. Tours: children with adults only.

Mansion, built in 1810 by George P. Macculloch, engineer for the Morris Canal, is restored and refurnished as a museum, with furniture, glass, silver, and china of the period.

From Rte. 202, westbound; right on Macculloch Ave., just short of Morristown center. Mansion is 2 blocks farther, on right.

ACORN HALL

68 Morris Avenue, Morristown, N.J.

Hours: by appointment; write Morris County Historical Society, P.O. Box 170, Morristown, N.J. 07960. Admission free.

Fine example of Victorial Italianate architecture. Interior and exterior unaltered since construction in 1853. Parlor suite in one elegant room once belonged to William Henry Harrison. House is Historical Society headquarters.

On Morris Ave., west of intersection with Columbia Road; near Governor Morris Inn.

SCHUYLER-HAMILTON HOUSE

5 Olyphant Pl., Morristown, N.J. 07960   Tel.: (201) JE 9-0656

Hours: Tues. and Fri., 10–12, 2–5. Admission free. Small children with adults only. Tours: groups of 6 or more by prearrangement.

Eighteenth Century house, authentically furnished as Colonial home, by Morristown Chapter, D.A.R. Here Betsy Schuyler met Alexander Hamilton. House now Chapter headquarters.

From Morristown center; right on Morris Ave. Second left beyond railroad underpass.

PASSAIC RIVER PARK

River Rd., Chatham Township, N.J.

County park containing softball field; picnic areas. Fishing in Passaic River.

THE POTTERY SHOP: THE OLD BONNELL HOUSE

32–34 Watchung Ave., Chatham, N.J. 07928   Tel.: (201) 635-6777

Hours: Pottery operates Monday through Saturday, 9:00–5:00. Admission free.

One of the few operating potteries in the area. Visitors are invited to watch the craftsmen making stoneware and to visit the "Old Bonnell House" which serves as a display background for the ware. Built about 1750, house was the homestead of the Bonnell family (Chatham was originally called Bonnell Town). Mrs. Bonnell baked bread for the Revolutionary soldiers, stepping over their sleeping bodies on the kitchen floor.

THE SPEEDWELL VILLAGE
Speedwell Avenue, Morris Plains, N.J.

Hours: by appointment. (For further information, write C. B. Scherzer, 13 Colles Ave., Morristown, N.J. 07960)

Historic restoration includes the Vail Homestead and barn where Samuel F. B. Morse invented the telegraph and where Alfred Vail perfected the code known as "Morse."

Route 53, north of Morristown.

GROVER CLEVELAND BIRTHPLACE
207 Bloomfield Ave., Caldwell, N.J. 07006   Tel.: (201) 226-1810

Hours: Tues.–Sat., 10–12, 1–5; Sun., 2–5. Fee: adults, 25¢; children under 12, free; school groups, free. Tour: reservations required.

Memorial to only U.S. President born in N.J.; 4 rooms of his furnishings and mementos of the period. Fascinating 19th century kitchen. Luncheon facilities nearby.

From Garden State Parkway, Exit 148; west on Bloomfield Ave. to Caldwell.

SALTBOX HOUSE
Main Street, Ledgewood, N.J. 07852

Hours: by appointment; write Roxbury Township Historical Society. Admission free. Tours: school groups and children accompanied by adults.

Restoration of New England style "saltbox" by Morris County Historical Society. Beam ceiling, windows and fireplace are of special interest.

South of Ledgewood traffic circle, junction of Rtes. 10 and 46.

THE TOURNE
Boonton, N.J.

Hours: daily, daylight hours. Admission free.

Morris County park with superb views of woodland. Rugged wooded area; nature and wildflower trails. Picnic tables; fireplaces; sledding. Limited overnight camping.

From Boonton center, follow signs to Riverside Hospital on Powerville Rd. The Tourne is opposite on left.

SOUTH MOUNTAIN RESERVATION
Millburn, Maplewood, West Orange, N.J.   Tel.: (201) 482-6400
Hours: daily. Admission free.

Largest Essex County reservation. Archery range; baseball diamonds; cross-country run; fishing. Bird watching; almost 20 miles of walking trails. Coasting areas; deer paddock; picnic areas; Scout camps. Bridle trails (20.6 miles); ski slopes and trails; hours, fees; telephone (201) 482-6400.

Turtle Back Zoo
Northfield Ave., West Orange, N.J.   Tel.: (201) 482-6400

Hours: daily, 10–6; weekends and holidays, 10–8; open May–Sept. Fee: adults, 50¢; children accompanied by adults, 25¢. Tours: groups by reservation.

Over 500 animals of 200 different species. Third largest collection of turtles and tortoises in the U.S. Tame animals to pet; scenic train ride; Eating House; picnic grove; free parking.

Deer Preserve—South Mountain Reservation
Crest Drive, Maplewood, N.J.

Hours: daily, Mar.–Oct. Admission free.

Abundance of tame deer in natural habitat. Delightful for small children. Snack bar provides deer "crackerjack."

SOUTH MOUNTAIN ARENA

560 Northfield Ave., West Orange, N.J.   Tel.: (201) 731-3828

Hours: open for public skating from September to May. End of June–late Aug., limited open sessions. Fee: admission, $1.25; skate rental, 70¢.

Large, well-equipped skating arena, seats over 2,600. Private, group instruction available. Regular hockey games, several ice shows each season.

On Rte. 508 (Northfield Ave.) in West Orange.

EAGLE ROCK RESERVATION

West Orange, Verona and Montclair, N.J.   Tel.: (201) 482-6400

Hours: daily. Admission free.

Lookout area provides superb view of New York skyline from Geo. Washington Bridge to the Verrazano Bridge. Baseball diamond; lookouts; bird watching; picnic areas; walking trails (3.5 miles). Almost 7 miles of bridle trails; ski trail; telephone for fees, times.

PAPERMILL PLAYHOUSE

Brookside Drive, Millburn, N.J. 07041   Tel.: (201) 376-4343

Hours: phone for program, hours and reservations; open all year. Tickets: prices vary.

Old paper mill converted into modern theater. Popular plays and musicals with Broadway stars. Ample parking. Special children's programs usually twice a month. Write for schedule.

From Millburn Ave., Millburn center; northeast on Old Short Hills Rd. Bear right at Brookside Drive, 2 blocks farther.

EDISON NATIONAL HISTORICAL SITES

Laboratory

Main St. and Lakeside Ave., West Orange, N.J. 07052   Tel.: (201) 736-0550

Hours: Daily, 9:30–4:30; closed Thanksgiving, Christmas, New Year's Days. Fee: adults, 50¢; children under 16, free. School groups free. Tours: guided tour for groups with advance reservations only.

Edison's original laboratory and workshop, plus many of his inventions; the original phonograph; reproductions of incandescent lights and of the first motion picture studio. Old movies shown. Parking nearby.

From Garden State Parkway, Exit 145 or 147; west on Park Ave. to Main St.; follow signs.

Glenmount

Glen Ave., Llewellyn Park, West Orange, N.J. 07052   Tel.: (201) 736-0550

Hours: Mon.–Sat., 10–4; closed Sundays and holidays. Fee: 50¢; must buy ticket at Laboratory. Guided tours one hour; no large groups on Saturday; tours limited to maximum of 20 persons.

Mansion where Edison lived, 1886–1931, with 2 floors of his furnishings, memorabilia, and library. No picnicking at either site.

Ask directions at the Laboratory.

NEW JERSEY FIRE MUSEUM
177 Valley St., South Orange, N.J. 07079   Tel.: (201) 763-1212
Hours: daily, except Sun., 10–5. Closed July, Aug. Fee: adults, $1.00; children under 15, 50¢. Group tours: by appointment only.

Authentic firehouse settings of 1850's, life-size speaking manne-quins; scale dioramas of early firehouses; animated diorama: "Burning of Chicago"; firefighting antiques; 11 hand-drawn engines. Guides dressed in old-time uniforms. Ages 7 up.

From Garden State Parkway, South Orange Ave. exit; to Valley St., turn left; 2 blocks; or Springfield Ave. exit to Valley Street, right turn; about 2 miles.

CENTERVILLE & SOUTHWESTERN RAILROAD ON THE BECKER FARM
Livingston Ave., Roseland, N.J. 07068   Tel.: (201) 226-2003
Hours: May 30–Labor Day, Sat. & Holidays; also Wed. during July and Aug. Fee: adults, 50¢; children under 12, 25¢. Write for brochure, schedule.

Miniature steam railroad with authentic equipment; 2-mile round trip. Ride through woods, farm. Visit working farm. For all ages.

On Rte. 527 between Livingston & Caldwell.

STERLING FOREST GARDENS
Tuxedo Park, N.Y. 10987   Tel.: (914) 351-2163
Hours: 11 to dusk, daily. Call for information on skiing. Entrance and parking fees; fees for skiing vary.

Largest landscaped floral park in U.S., featuring different display as season changes. Flamingoes, peacocks, swans, native birds. Space Age children's playground, refreshment patios, and International Pavilion with restaurant, sidewalk cafe, gift shop. Scenic train to gardens. Skiing: open all week during winter.

Palisades Interstate Parkway to Rte. 210, 3 miles to gardens.

GREENWOOD LAKE
Hewitt, N.J.
Hours: daily, all year.

Good fishing, ice skating, ice boating. Swimming spots with picnic areas on Macopin Road, West Milford. (Bubbling Spring Lake and Green Valley Park, open June–Aug.) Boat rentals.

Rte. 23 northwest from Rte. 46. At Riverdale traffic circle, Rte. 519 to Hewitt.

MUSEUM VILLAGE OF SMITH'S CLOVE

Monroe, N.Y. 10950   Tel.: (914) 782-8405

Hours: 10–5, April 15–June 14 & Sept. 3–Oct. 31; June 15–Sept. 2, 10–6. Saturdays and Sundays, 10–6. Fee: adults, $2.00; children 6–15, 75¢; groups, 20 or more, adults, $1.25; children, 55¢. One adult per 12 children, free. Groups by reservation.

This entire village is a museum, showing the way people lived from the days of homespun to the end of the 19th century. One entrance–exit; large farm, railroad equipment for youngsters to climb. Refreshments and rest rooms; picnic tables.

From N.Y. Thruway Exit 16; west 4½ miles on Rtes. 6 & 17 to Exit 129 (Museum Village Rd.).

DEY MANSION

Preakness Valley Park, Totowa Rd., Wayne Township, N.J. Tel.: (201) 696-1766

Hours: Tues., Wed., Fri., 1–5; weekends, 10–5. Fee: over 16, 50¢. Tour: 40 minutes.

Georgian house built 1740, restored 1934. 18th-century furniture. Attic is small museum. On second and fourth Saturdays, 1–4 P.M., Colonial Debs demonstrate one or more early American crafts. Public golf course in Preakness Valley Park; garden with picnic tables.

From south, Garden State Exit 153B; from north, Exit 154. From Rte. 46, exit at Preakness, pass Totowa Airport to fork (Preakness Dairy on left), bear right, about half mile on Totowa Road.

RINGWOOD STATE PARK

R.D. Ringwood, N.J. 07456   Tel.: (201) 962-7031

This state park includes historic and recreational interests.

Ringwood Manor House

78-room house, originally home of Robert Erskine and later property of Cooper and Hewitt families, is now a museum. Antique furnishings, firearms, implements and relics. Lake, mill pond, blacksmith shop, formal gardens, picnic area.

Shepherd Lake

Facilities for bathing, boating, fishing, hiking, picnicking, trap and skeet shooting, ice skating. Lodge offers cafeteria, snack bar. Boats, canoes may be rented.

From State Highway 23, to Rte. 513, at N.Y. State line.

The iron chain at Ringwood

THE MONTCLAIR ART MUSEUM

South Mountain and Bloomfield Avenues, Montclair, N.J. 07042
Tel.: (201) 746-5555

Hours: Tues.–Sat., 10–5; Sun., 2–5:30; closed Mondays and July–Aug. Admission free. Tours, gallery talks: call Education Dept.

Permanent collections: paintings, sculpture, principally American. Exhibitions change frequently. Japanese Girl's Doll Festival, March. Gallery Talks: Sundays, 3:30 P.M. (3 P.M. during concert season); Sunday afternoon concerts, November and March, 4 P.M.

From Garden State Parkway, Exit 148; north on Bloomfield Ave.

PATERSON MUSEUM (Natural History, Sciences and the Arts)

268 Summer Street, Paterson, N.J. 07501   Tel.: (201) 742-4820

Hours: Mon.–Fri., 1–5; Sat., 10–12 and 1–5. Admission free. Tour: approx. one hour.

Excellent small natural history, natural and physical sciences museum. Outstanding collection of minerals and gems from all over the world; comprehensive presentation of New Jersey minerals; large fluorescent rock display. No luncheon facilities but advance arrangements for out-of-town groups may be made at nearby YWCA ((201) 684-6406). Parking on museum lot.

Note: At nearby West Side Park see the Holland Submarine, first successful one, built in 1881.

From Garden State Parkway, Exit 156; north on Rte. 20, west on Broadway. Museum at Broadway and Summer St.

LAMBERT CASTLE (Historical Museum)

Garrett Mountain Reservation, Paterson, N.J.   Tel.: (201) 523-9883

Hours: Wed., Thurs., Fri., 1–4:45; weekends, 11–4:45. Admission free. Tour: guides available; large groups by reservation.

Spanish-American War documents, artifacts; antique machinery; household effects; firearms used in Passaic Valley; rooms copied from Warwick Castle, England. Reservation facilities include picknicking, fireplaces; ball fields; playground.

From Rte. 46, north on Valley Road about 2 miles.

LAZZARA BAKERY

Madison and Gett Ave., Paterson, N.J. 07561   Tel.: (201) 742-2424

Hours: by reservation only, weekdays. No fee. Tours for groups by reservation.

Large commercial bakery. Tour includes all steps in making bread. Each child is given a sample loaf. Rest room facilities not easily available. Diner across the street, and retail bakeshop with Lazzara products.

One block from Main St., Paterson.

ISRAEL CRANE HOUSE

110 Orange Road, Montclair, N.J. 07042   Tel.: (201) 783-4322

Hours: open to public Sun. only 2–5, except July–Aug. Other hours by appointment. Admission free. Special 5th grade student days: Tues. and Wed. afternoons, Jan.–March.

Historic house museum of the Montclair Historical Society. Federal-style mansion erected 1796, roof raised circa 1830. Large house with beautifully proportioned rooms, superb furniture and decorations, showing way of life of wealthy family of the period. Front parlor in 18th-century style; back parlor in Empire period. Museum Room has exhibits, changed periodically, on early Americana. School Room has old tools; dunce stool and hat; early wooden blackboard; lunch baskets; old school books. Extensive research material, prepared by the Montclair Junior League, available: Crane family, lighting, cooking, school, tour information, etc. School program: slide talk on life in early Crane Town; tour of house; cooking demonstration in restored kitchen. Kitchen features old utensils, fireplace oven, old reflector rotisserie; cooking demonstrations by costumed Docents. For schedule of special events and reservations, write Montclair Historical Society, Box 322, Montclair, N.J. 07042.

Garden State Parkway, Bloomfield Ave. exit; west about 3 miles to Orange Road; left.

Demonstrating colonial cooking, Israel Crane House. *D. J. Zehnder*

CLAIRIDGE THEATER

486 Bloomfield Ave., Montclair, N.J. 07042   Tel.: (201) 746-5564

Hours: evenings except Sun., 8:30; Sun., 7:30. Matinee, Sat., Sun., 2:30. Matinee during summer also.

1st run cinema house. Arrangements can be made for special showings of select motion pictures for student, other groups, clubs, etc. All projection processes including Cinerama.

On Bloomfield Ave., Montclair center.

BELLEVUE THEATER

268 Bellevue Ave., Upper Montclair, N.J. 07043   Tel.: (201) 744-1455

Hours: variable. Fees: vary with show.

Theater with modern projection, sound reproduction equipment. First-run foreign, domestic films, from 4 weeks to 3 months each. Parking; eating facilities nearby. Theater parties for fund-raising organizations may be arranged.

From Rte. 46, eastbound; south on Valley Rd., Clifton; right on Bellevue Ave.

MILLS RESERVATION

Cedar Grove and Montclair, N.J.

Hours: daily. Admission free.

Natural woodlands with excellent view of New York City. Heavily wooded, preserved in natural state; among many varieties of trees to be found are aspen and pin cherry. Burnt over area points up excellent example of forest succession. Bird watching; walking trails.

MOUNTAINSIDE PARK

500 Upper Mountain Ave., Upper Montclair, N.J.   Tel.: (201) PI 4-3693

Hours: daily, tennis: daily, 10–8, May–Nov. Admission free. Tennis: weekdays, 25¢ per hour; Sun. and holidays, 50¢ per hour.

Park facilities include: 10 clay tennis courts, lessons available in summer; baseball fields; children's playground. In winter, organized sledding and skating. Bird sanctuary in wooded area. Presby Iris Gardens display over 1,000 varieties, from about May 1.

From junction of Rte. 23 and Bloomfield Ave., Verona; southeast on Bloomfield: left on Upper Mountain Ave.

HIGHGATE GALLERY (Art)

50 Upper Montclair Plaza, Upper Montclair, N.J. 07043 Tel.: (201) 746-6883

Hours: Tues.–Sat., 12:30–4:30; Sun., 3–5. Closed June 15–Labor Day. Admission free.

Accredited gallery of contemporary American art.

From Rte. 46, eastbound; south on Valley Rd., Clifton; right on Bellevue Ave. Behind Bellevue Theater.

NUTLEY WALKING TOUR (historic houses)

A tour of 6 historic houses in Nutley, all within easy walking distance of one another, may be of interest to groups. These are not usually open to the public; for special arrangements call (201) NO 7-1080, or write Women's Club, 226 Chestnut St., Nutley, N.J. 07110.

> Abraham and Warren Vreeland House (1838)
> 51 Enclosure
> Feland House (early 1800's)
> 63 Enclosure
> Methodist Parsonage (1700's)
> 213 Passaic Ave.
> Captain Speer House (1760)
> 149 Church St.
> John Mason House (1812)
> Calico Lane
> Vreeland Homestead (Women's Club) (1702)
> 226 Chestnut St.

From Garden State Parkway, northbound, Exit 151; right on East Passaic Ave.; left on Centre St. to Franklin Ave.; left to Church St.

NUTLEY HISTORICAL SOCIETY, MUSEUM

65 Church St., Nutley, N.J. 07110 Tel.: (201) NO 7-7892, Miss Ann Troy

Hours: Sun., 2–5; other days by reservation only. Admission free.

Originally a schoolhouse, built 1875. Contains Annie Oakley collection; Civil, Spanish-American Wars, World Wars I and II mementos; N.J. birds; rocks and minerals.

From Garden State Parkway, northbound, Exit 151; right on East Passaic Ave.; left on Centre St. to Franklin Ave.; left to Church St. Turn left.

SCIENTIFIC GLASS APPARATUS CO., INC.
735 Broad St., Bloomfield, N.J. 07003   Tel.: (201) 748-6600

Hours: Mon.–Fri., 8–4:45 by reservation only, apply 2–3 weeks in advance. Admission free. Tour: guides available for groups high school age and up, one hour.

Glass tubing factory. Laboratory equipment such as condensors, beakers, graduates, thermometers. Glass blowing but not on decorative objects. Lunch facilities in nearby Bloomfield center.

From Bloomfield Center, take Broad St., northbound. Located on Broad St. between Bay and Watchung Ave.

BLOOMFIELD HISTORICAL SOCIETY
90 Broad St., Bloomfield, N.J. 07003

Hours: Wed., 1–5. Groups by appointment. Admission free.

Many pre-Revolutionary items and historical artifacts; old oils; excellent collection of mid-18th-century costumes.

On 2nd floor of Bloomfield Free Public Library Annex.

WATSESSING PARK
Bloomfield Ave. and Glenwood Ave., Bloomfield, N.J.   Tel.: (201) 482-6400

Hours: daily. Admission free.

County park's name derived from Lenni Lenape Indians' words for hill (watschu) and stone (assan). Baseball diamonds; lighted basketball court; ice skating (natural ice); lawn bowling greens; running track; soccer fields. PAL center. Playgrounds.

Garden State Parkway Exit 148; west on Bloomfield Ave. to first light.

BROOKDALE REFORMED DUTCH CHURCH
10 Bellevue Ave., Bloomfield, N.J. 07003   Tel.: (201) 338-7676

Hours: by reservation only. Admission free.

Small Colonial-style church, built 1882. Adjoining churchyard with many headstones of old Dutch settlers of area. Lunch facilities nearby, or picnicking in Brookdale Park.

Bloomfield Ave. northbound to Glen Ridge. Bear right on Broad St.; pass Brookdale Park to Bellevue Ave.

BROOKDALE PARK

Bloomfield and Montclair, N.J. Tel.: (201) 482-6400

Hours: daily. Admission free.

Third largest Essex County park. Handsome rose garden; variety of plant material not indigenous to the area. Activities include: archery; baseball diamonds; bicycling; coasting area; football field; ice skating (natural ice); model boat sailing; picnic area; playground; running track; soccer field; tennis courts.

Garden State Parkway, northbound, Exit 151; east on Watchung Ave. past Broad St. intersection. Entrance on right.

TETERBORO AIRPORT

Rte. 46, Teterboro, N.J. 07608 Tel.: (201) 288-1776 (Pan American World Airways)

Tours: by appointment only, children, 3rd grade and up. Admission free. Open every day.

In addition to the tour, visitors may take short rides in planes owned by two independent companies. Fee, generally $5.00. Hours: 9–sunset. Arrange in advance: Teterboro School of Aeronautics: 288-1880; General Aviation: 288-9734.

Rte. 46 west; from Garden State Parkway, or east from N.J. Turnpike.

PALISADES INTERSTATE PARK

New York and New Jersey Interstate Public Park system providing excellent recreational facilities. Stretches from Fort Lee, New Jersey, just south of George Washington Bridge, to Storm King Mountain, 50 miles north. Consists of a series of separate parks along the west bank of the Hudson River, all approachable from Palisades Interstate Parkway. Special features are described in the following section. The Parkway itself is a beautiful scenic drive following the Hudson River, then swerving inland and terminating at Bear Mountain Bridge.

TALLMAN MOUNTAIN STATE PARK

Rte. 9W, Sparkill, N.Y.

Hours: Opening, closing dates vary each season. Fee for parking, swimming.

Bathhouse and locker facilities, swimming pool, wading pool. Hiking trails and picnic areas.

Rte. 9W to entrance just south of Sparkill, N.Y.

ENGLEWOOD BOAT BASIN

Englewood Cliffs, N.J.   Tel.: (201) 568-9510

Open weekends, holidays during spring and fall; daily during summer. Fee for parking.

Several picnic areas with picnic tables, charcoal grills, and refreshment stands. Trails along Hudson River and steep climb to upper roadway. Suggest taking scenic Henry Hudson Drive from George Washington Bridge, past Englewood Boat Basin and terminating at Alpine Boat Basin.

Exit 1 from Palisades Interstate Parkway or Rte. 9W to Palisade Ave. turnoff.

GREENBROOK SANCTUARY (birds)

Rte. 9W, Tenafly, N.J.   Tel.: (201) 768-1360

Hours: by appointment only. Call or write Palisades Nature Association, Box 203, Englewood, N.J. 07631. Fee: $10.00 per group tour of 20.

Conducted tour through well-preserved sanctuary. Magnificent views of Hudson River. Conservation of trees, shrubs natural to area, especially attractive to birds.

From George Washington Bridge north on Rte. 9W. Gate is opposite Clinton Ave. turnoff to Tenafly.

ALPINE BOAT BASIN

Alpine, N.J.   Tel.: (201) 768-1360

Open weekends, holidays during spring and fall; daily during summer. Fee for parking.

Picnic areas with tables, fireplaces, pavilion; old Cornwallis House; trails.

Exit 2 from Palisades Interstate Parkway, or Rte. 9W to Palisades Interstate Park Headquarters, N.J. section.

Stony Point Battleground

STONY POINT BATTLEFIELD RESERVATION

Stony Point, N.Y.

Hours: April 12–Oct., 8–sunset. Museum: open 9–4:30 weekdays, 9:30–6 weekends. Admission free. Restrictions: must walk through Park, no roads, basket picnics only, no fireplaces.

Lovely grounds, breathtaking view, flowering dogwood late in May. Children like old cannons, reliving famous storming of Stony Point by General "Mad Anthony" Wayne.

PERKINS MEMORIAL DRIVE

Fee. Starts near Bear Mountain Inn. Connects Rte. 9W and Palisades Interstate Parkway and goes to top of Bear Mountain and Observation Building. Beautiful views of Hudson River and highlands. Picnic area on summit of mountain.

BEAR MOUNTAIN STATE PARK

Northernmost section of Palisades Interstate Park located at junction of Rte. 6 and Palisades Interstate Parkway. Main entrance to Park is at Bear Mountain Bridge. Most day recreational facilities are concentrated here near Park entrance but there are some 60 square miles of wooded area in Bear Mountain and Harriman Sections. Information Center at Bear Mountain Inn. For group outings write Bear Mountain State Park, Bear Mountain, N.Y. 10911, or phone (914) 786-2701 for information and permits.

BEAR MOUNTAIN INN

Located at Park entrance. Main tourist center with snack bar, lounges, restaurant, overnight facilities. Large parking facilities. In summer—steamer landing, swimming pools, boating lakes, playing fields, roller skating rink, Saturday night dancing, square dancing twice weekly, tennis courts, bridle paths, zoo, and nature museum. In winter—toboggan slide, ski runs, ice rink, skating at Lake Hessian, and ski jump tournaments.

Molly Pitcher Monument, West Point

WEST POINT, UNITED STATES MILITARY ACADEMY

Rte. 218 (Storm King Highway), West Point, N.Y.

Hours: daily. Admission free.

West Point Reservation covers 15,000 acres overlooking Hudson River. Highlights are cadet parades in May, and in Sept. through early Oct., Mon., Tues., Thurs., 5:30 P.M.; Sat., 1:10 P.M. On home football game days Sat. parade is 11:30 A.M. Plebe parades Mon., Wed., Fri. at 5 P.M.; Sat. at 9 A.M. from last week in July to third week in Aug. No parades or reviews on Sundays. Ceremonies cancelled in bad weather.

Points of interest include Cadet Chapel, Battle Monument, Academy Museum, Library, restored Fort Putnam, Michie Stadium. Visitors' Information Center open Apr. to Oct. located at Thayer Gate and features displays of cadet training, typical cadet room and free movies. Hotel on reservation grounds with restaurant facilities open to public. Also snack bar and picnic tables available.

HARRIMAN STATE PARK

This section is also part of Palisades Interstate Park and is contiguous to Bear Mountain Inn. In addition to wooded area for camping and fishing the following special features should be noted:

Lake Tiorati

Picnic area and bathing beach.

Lake Sebago

Roller skating, picnic areas, swimming, boating, lockers, archery tournaments.

Silver Mine Ski Area

Artificial snow with 4 slopes.

Anthony Wayne Recreation Area

Large swimming pools and picnic area. Free parking. Swimming fee. Empire State Music Festival during summer.

SLEEPY HOLLOW RESTORATIONS

For information on the following listings write Sleepy Hollow Restorations, Inc., Box 245, Tarrytown, N.Y. 10591. The corpora-

Washington Irving's Home. *Sleepy Hollow Restorations*

tion is a nonprofit educational foundation responsible for the restoration and maintenance of the three historic sites. Hours and fees are the same for each. Hours: Mon.–Fri., April 1–Nov. 15, 10–5. Mon.–Fri., Nov. 16–Mar. 31, 12–4; weekends, year-round, 10–5. Closed Thanksgiving, Christmas, New Year's days. Fees: adults, $1.50; children 6–14, 75¢. Family and group rates; special school rates. Groups must make advance reservations.

Sunnyside (Washington Irving's home)

Rte. 9, Tarrytown, N.Y.

The house reflects the personal tastes of the author and is a singular, charming mélange of architecture: it began as a small 1-story stone cottage built in the late 1600's and Irving added to it after buying it in 1835. The house contains Irving's library, personal effects and furniture. Since it remained in the Irving family until the late 1930's, it is considered one of the best-documented historic houses in the country. The 20-acre estate surrounding the house contains an icehouse with a church steeple and "Little Mediterranean," a beautiful small pond used as the estate's reservoir. Picnic tables; soft drinks but no food sold. Special programs: write for information.

From N.Y. Thruway, cross Tappan Zee Bridge; take first exit (Rte. 9); south on Rte. 9 one mile to W. Sunnyside Lane.

Van Cortlandt Manor

Croton-On-Hudson, N.Y.

Built in 1680, this handsome manor became the permanent home of the Van Cortlandts about 1749, and so remained for about two hundred years. The first dweller was Pierre Van Cortlandt who became first Lt. Governor of New York State. The exterior and interior restored to the era of the late 18th century. The manor contains original family furnishings, notably porcelain and pewter collections. The red brick Lawn Walk, about 750 feet and bordered by flowering trees and beds, leads to the Ferry House and Kitchen. The Ferry House contains a Bar Room with beautiful pewters, and a Common Room. The Kitchen, which provided food for travelers crossing the river, is notable for its beehive oven. There are picnic tables but only soft drinks are sold.

After crossing Tappan Zee Bridge, take first exit (Rte. 9) and go north on Rte. 9 about nine miles. Follow signs.

Oak-timbered dam. Philipsburg Manor. *Sleepy Hollow Restorations*

Stringing dried apples, Van Cortlandt Manor. *Sleepy Hollow Restorations*

Philipsburg Manor, Upper Mills

North Tarrytown, N.Y.

This restoration was an early 1700's gristmill-trading center complex: northern headquarters for the Philips family's 90,000-acre land holding. The Manor House, a 2-story stone house, was completed in 1720 and is restored and outfitted in that period. Reconstructed on the original site, the gristmill is an operating, water-powered mill. An oak-timbered, 250-foot dam is topped by a walkway. The estate contains a reception building built by the Restoration to provide information about the family and the period; theater, exhibition room; lunchroom is available only by reservation; no other eating facilities.

Cross Tappan Zee Bridge, take first exit (Rte. 9) and go north on Rte. 9 about two miles.

WASHINGTON MASONIC SHRINE (DE WINT HOUSE)

Oak Tree Road, Tappan, N.Y.   Tel.: (914) EL 9-1359

Hours: daily, 9–4. Admission free.

One of the oldest houses in Rockland County. Washington's headquarters during the trial of Major John André; also meeting place for Washington and the British when they signed the agreement on the evacuation of New York City. Within the grounds is the Old Dutch Reformed Church where the trial of Major André was held. The nearby manse (privately owned) is the oldest manse in continuous use since it was built. Lunch may be had in the 1776 House nearby, where Major André was held before his trial, then, as now, a tavern.

From Palisades Interstate Parkway, just beyond N.J. border; south on Rte. 303 to Oak Tree Rd. stop light, then west to Shrine. Continue on Oak Tree Rd., bearing right, to 1776 House.

GARDEN STATE PLAZA CIVIC AUDITORIUM

Garden State Plaza Shopping Center, Lower Level of Concourse, Rtes. 4 and 17, Paramus, N.J.   Tel.: (201) 843-3690

Admission free.

Programs for entire year, many planned expressly for children from preschool through 8th grade. Annual events: Lollipops Concerts (four Saturdays prior to arrival of Santa Claus); Christmas Week shows (marionettes); Summer Movie Festival. For programs, see area newspapers.

BERGEN COUNTY PARKS

CAMPGAW MOUNTAIN COUNTY RESERVATION

Campgaw Rd., Mahwah, Franklin Lakes, Oakland, N.J.

Hours: open all year; for information on skiing, tobogganing call Bergen County Park Commission (201) 447-4660. For camping permits, write or visit in advance, Bergen County Park Commission, 575 Main Street, Hackensack, N.J. 07601. Fees: vary.

Reservation features nature trails, picnic tables, fireplaces, shelter. Overnight camping sites (some with tent platforms or adirondack shelters; some accessible to trailers); play equipment; visitors' center: lounge, snacks; bridle trail for permit holders; comfort station; ranger service.

Off Rte. 202. Follow signs.

Campgaw Mountain Ski Center

Hours: winter months; weekdays, 10–10; weekends, holidays, 2 p.m.–10. No Sunday night skiing. Fees: vary.

1,650 foot main slope with chair lift; 600 foot school slope with T-bar lift. Machine-made snow; shelter in visitor's center: snacks, equipment sales and rentals.

Campgaw Mountain Toboggan Chutes

Adjacent to ski slopes. Same time as ski center.

Artificially iced, about 1,100 feet. Warming building; refreshment area. Rentals; private equipment must meet specifications.

DARLINGTON COUNTY PARK
Mahwah and Ramsey, N.J.

Hours: closed Dec., Jan., Feb., Mar. Fees: entrance fee during swimming season: Memorial Day–Labor Day; swimming fees vary.

Three lakes: 2 for swimming, 1 for fishing and rental boating. Field house: snack bar. Locker rooms, pavilion, comfort station; playground; picnic tables. Facilities include: tennis; handball; volleyball; softball; shuffleboard; basketball; horseshoes. For season permits write park commission.

From Rte. 202; east onto Darlington Ave. in Mahwah.

BERGEN COUNTY WILDLIFE CENTER
Crescent Ave., Wyckoff, N.J.

Hours: daily, 8 A.M. to ½ hour after sunset, all year. (Open to 11 P.M. for group with meeting permit.) Admission free. Children must be accompanied by adult.

This remarkable center features waterfowl pond; nature walk; window wall overlooking pond, with binoculars; console of lighted color photographs; nature exhibits in skylighted display hall; indoor pool planting and terrariums; live fish, frogs, turtles, bees, snakes, lizards, other woodland creatures; nature slides with sound-track commentary in viewing corridor; browsing library; naturalists in attendance; rock collection; live animal and bird shelters; deer. Wooded picnic area. Field trips may be scheduled for school classes and clubs: illustrated talks and guided nature tours. Chaperons must accompany children. Permit requests 2 weeks in advance: write or call Bergen County Wildlife Center, Crescent Ave., Wyckoff, N.J. 07481. Tel.: (201) 891-5571. Summer classes for grades 1–6.

On Crescent Ave. between Rtes. 208 and 17.

ROCKLEIGH BERGEN COUNTY GOLF COURSE
Rockleigh, Northvale, Norwood, N.J.

27 holes; field house with pro shop, snack bar.

Rochelle Park Area
Facilities include ice skating rink; playground; picnic tables, fireplaces.

Saddle Brook Area

Facilities: lake with duck feeding; fishing; model speedboat racing and model boat sailing. Baseball; football; playground; ice skating; picnic tables, fireplaces; bicycle, pedestrian path around lake; horseshoes.

Wild Duck Pond Area

Ridgewood

Pond with ice skating, duck feeding, model boat sailing, fishing. Picnic tables and fireplaces; shuffleboard; horseshoes; playground; recreation room; comfort station.

Tower Restoration

Arcola, Paramus

Tower and paddle wheel in Easton gardens; near site of historic 1745 Red Mill.

South of Rte. 4, from Saddle River and Paramus Roads.

SADDLE RIVER COUNTY PARK

Dunkerhook Area

Paramus

Picnic tables and fireplaces, 2 picnic shelters; duck feeding; playground; horseshoes; comfort station.

Glen Rock Area

Lake with duck feeding, fishing, model boat sailing. Picnic tables and fireplaces; play equipment; ice skating. Comfort station.

Rochelle Park Area

Ice skating rink; playground; picnic tables and fireplaces.

VAN SAUN COUNTY PARK

Paramus and River Edge, N.J.

Children's zoo; children's railroad; walk-through aviary; re-created 1860's farm scene. 12-court tennis center with field house, practice backstop. Picnic tables, fireplaces, shelters. Garden around Washington Spring. Pony rides. Horseback riding lessons. Duck feeding; shuffleboard; horseshoes; play equipment. Lake with fishing, ice skating. Sledding; ballfields; comfort station; refreshment stand.

Aviary, Van Saun County Park

OVERPECK COUNTY PARK

Teaneck, Englewood, Leonia, Palisades Park, Ridgefield Park, N.J.

Overpeck Bergen County Golf Course

18 holes; field house with lounge, snack bar, deck, pro shop.

Leonia Section

Family recreations: baseball; picnic tables and fireplaces; ice skating rink.

Palisades Park Section

Athletic fields.

RIVERSIDE COUNTY PARK

North Area

Lyndhurst

Picnic tables, fireplaces, shelter; ice skating rink; baseball, softball, football; tennis courts; playground. Ballfield with lights and bleachers for 1,600.

South Area

North Arlington and Lyndhurst

Children's playground; family recreations.

TRICKER'S WATER GARDENS

East Allendale Rd., Saddle River, N.J. 07458   Tel.: (201) 327-0721

Hours: daily except Sun., 8–5; year round. Admission free.

America's oldest water gardens. Large displays of water lilies; goldfish; tropical fish; aquarium plants.

North on Rte. 17, to Saddle River turnoff. ½ mile to town center.

Zabriskie House

ZABRISKIE (VON STEUBEN) HOUSE
(Historical Museum)

New Bridge Rd., River Edge, N.J. 07661   Tel.: (201) 487-1739

Hours: daily except Mon., 10–12, 1–5; Sun., 2–5. Fee: adults, 25¢; children under 12, free. Tour: reservation for group required.

Main building erected in 1739, addition in 1752. Occupied by British and Americans during Revolution. Given to Baron von Steuben by New Jersey in payment of nation's debt. Early American furnishings, costumes, Indian artifacts, and a dugout canoe.

Rte. 4 to Main St., Hackensack, north to New Bridge, then right to end of street.

SCHOOLHOUSE MUSEUM
PARAMUS HISTORICAL AND PRESERVATION SOCIETY

650 East Glen Ave. (at Rte. 17), Ridgewood, N.J. 07450

Hours: Wed. or historical holiday, 2:30–4:30. Call to see if open: (201) 445-1778, or (201) 447-3242. Sun., 3–5 (weather permitting, winter months). Admission free. Tours: groups by appointment only; call (201) 652-7425.

Built in 1873, the building maintains schoolroom atmosphere, as well as depicting the manner and mode of living from colonial times to the 19th century in this once predominantly Dutch neighborhood. Exhibits of Indian relics and artifacts, spinning and weaving equipment, farm tools, harness, toys, dolls.

Old Paramus Reformed Church

Hours: included in tour of Museum, by appointment only. Admission free.

The original church, built in 1735, served as a barracks, hospital, prison, and headquarters for Gen. George Washington. Other historic figures here were Lt. Col. Alexander Hamilton, the Marquis de Lafayette, Col. Aaron Burr, Gen. Anthony Wayne, and Maj. Gen. Charles Lee, whose court martial for disobedience of orders at the Battle of Monmouth took place, in part, here. Continental Army encampment site and Revolutionary cemetery close by. Present church built in 1800.

NEWARK CHURCH TOUR

Four churches of historic and architectural interest are located in Newark. All four may be visited during a morning or afternoon; all are near good restaurants or Branch Brook Park for picnics.

Old First Church

820 Broad St., Newark, N.J.   Tel.: (201) 642-0260

Hours: daily. Admission free.

Picturesque church in beautiful grounds. Early American architecture.

Near intersection of Broad and Market Sts., Newark center.

Trinity Cathedral

Broad and Rector Sts., Newark, N.J.   Tel.: (201) 622-4306

Hours: daily. Admission free.

Colonial period church, built 1746. Box pews, interesting floor plan.

Directly opposite Hahne's Dep't Store.

North Reformed Church

510 Broad St., Newark, N.J.   Tel.: (201) 623-3198

Hours: Mon.–Fri., 9–4; by reservation only. Admission free.

Built 1859 in second period Gothic architecture. Exterior of locally quarried red sandstone; colorful memorial windows.

Broad St., facing Washington Park and next to Mutual Benefit Insurance Co.

Cathedral of the Sacred Heart

89 Ridge St., Newark, N.J.   Tel.: (201) 484-4600

Hours: daily. Admission free.

Beautiful cathedral, begun 1892. Notable mosaics depict life of Christ.

From Bloomfield Ave., southbound; right on Clinton Ave. Cathedral on right, one block farther.

BRANCH BROOK PARK

Newark and Belleville, N.J.   Tel.: (201) 482-6400

Hours: daily. Admission free.

First county park in the U.S. During Civil War Union troops trained here. Facilities include: baseball diamonds, bicycling, boating, bocce, coasting areas. Summer concert series; fishing; ice skating (natural ice); paddle boats. Also, cross-country run; cricket crease; football fields; Gaelic football field; horseshoe pitching; playground; senior citizens centers; soccer fields; tennis courts.

Enter from E. Bloomfield Ave., spur Rte. 506; from Park Ave., State Highway 16.

NEWARK PUBLIC LIBRARY

5 Washington St., Newark, N.J. 17102   Tel.: (201) 624-7100

Hours: Mon.–Fri., 9–9; Sat., 9–5. Admission free.

Exhibits of historical items; industrial displays; paintings and drawings, etc. Special film and story programs for children 6–12. Free monthly calendar of events on request.

NEWARK MUSEUM

43–49 Washington St., Newark, N.J. 17102   Tel.: (201) 642-0011

Hours: Mon.–Sat., 12–5; Sun. and holidays, 1–5. Admission free. Tour: special groups may make reservations through the Education Office.

Museum devoted to art, science and industry. Changing exhibits of fine collections of American painting and sculpture; decorative arts; Oriental arts; ethnology; natural sciences, etc. Junior Museum, Fire Museum and large Garden. Planetarium (adults 25¢; children 15¢): Sat., Sun. and holidays, 2 & 3 P.M., Sept. through June; Mon., Wed., Fri., 12:15, July & Aug.

On Washington Street opposite Washington Park.

NEWARK FIRE MUSEUM

In the garden of the Newark Museum, 43–49 Washington St., Newark, N.J.   Tel.: (201) 642-0011

Hours: Mon.–Fri., 12–3; Sat., 12–4:30; Sun. and holidays, 1–4:30. Admission free. Tours: weekdays; groups by reservation through Museum's Education Office.

Collection of objects relating to fire-fighting, past and present, with particular reference to the city of Newark. Engines, helmets, other equipment; photographs, paintings, documents. Displayed in carriage house once belonging to Marcus L. Ward, Governor of New Jersey after the Civil War, and member of Newark's Hook and Ladder #1. Currently maintained by the Newark Fire Department Historical Association.

Atop the old pumper, Newark Fire Museum

NEWARK AIRPORT
PORT NEWARK/ELIZABETH
Route 1, New Jersey Turnpike Exit 14, Newark, N.J. Tel.: (201) 344-8200 for reservations.

Tours daily except Saturday and Sunday by advance reservation only. No charge for tour. Group must provide bus for use on tour. Group size 25–50. For adults and over 8.

Airport tour includes passenger and cargo terminals, service areas, and advantageous view of takeoff and landing areas. Aircraft entered when airline schedules permit. Adult tours include inspection of $200 million redevelopment project.

Seaport tours include view of all types of maritime cargo handling—lumber, automobiles, salt, scrap, general cargo and container ship operations at the world's largest container port.

WEEQUAHIC PARK
Newark, N.J. Tel.: (201) 482-6400

Hours: daily. Admission free.

Lake in this county park for boating, fishing; other facilities include baseball diamonds; lighted basketball courts; cross-country run; football fields; 18-hole golf course; ice skating (natural ice); soccer; tennis; playgrounds, a rose garden, and picnic grounds.

ANHEUSER-BUSCH, INC. (Brewery)

200 U.S. Rte. 1, Newark, N.J. 17114   Tel.: (201) 248-3200

Hours: weekdays, 10–11, 1:15, 2:15, 3:15, 4:15; evenings, groups by reservation. Admission free. Tour: for high school age and up, one adult for each 8 students.

A division of America's largest brewery. Tour shows step-by-step beer processing. Beer seen in fermentation stage only, but all equipment used in process is on view.

From Rte. 1, southbound; plant is on right, between Newark and Elizabeth. Public Service Buses #132, 134 and 43 stop at Administration Building.

NEW JERSEY HISTORICAL SOCIETY

230 Broadway, Newark, N.J. 17104   Tel.: (201) 483-3939

Hours: Tues.–Sat., 10–4:30. Admission free.

Displays show N.J. culture from earliest development. Public reference library; field trips; lectures available.

From Broad St., Newark, northbound; left after D. L. & W. Railroad underpass.

1875 kitchen, New Jersey Historical Society

WASHINGTON COUNTY PARK
North St., Jersey City, N.J.

Hours: daylight. Admission free. Fees: tennis, swimming.

Large swimming pool, 200' x 75'. Tennis courts; baseball; basketball; playgrounds; picnicking.

From Rtes. 1 & 9: east onto Patterson Plank Rd. which divides park.

LINCOLN COUNTY PARK
Jersey City, N.J.

Hours: daylight. Admission free; fees for tennis.

Formal flower beds; beautiful fountain. Facilities include children's playground; tennis courts; track; baseball; archery; sledding slopes. Model-boat sailing on lake. Restaurant.

From N.J. Turnpike, east to Jersey City; left on Hudson Blvd. Main entrance on Belmont Ave.

BAYONNE COUNTY PARK
Bayonne, N.J.

Hours: daylight. Admission free; fee for tennis.

Park with natural forest; 10 clay tennis courts; athletic field and track; playground; children's wading pools. View Newark Bay and Airport activity. Picnic tables.

Park is on Hudson Blvd.

WEST HUDSON COUNTY PARK
Schuyler Ave., Harrison, N.J.

Park facilities feature basketball; ice skating (natural ice); baseball; playgrounds. No picnicking.

From Harrison Boulevard, north on Schuyler Ave.

NORTH HUDSON COUNTY PARK
78th Street and Bergenline Ave., North Bergen, N.J.

Hours: daylight. Fee for tennis; boat rentals.

Park facilities include ice skating; tennis; boating (rentals); fishing; playgrounds; baseball; basketball; picnicking.

From Rtes. 1 & 9: east on 78th Street to Bergenline Ave.

HIRAM BLAUVELT WILDLIFE MUSEUM

637 Kinderkamack Rd., Oradell, N.J. 07649 Tel.: (201) 261-0012

Hours: 10–3, Thurs. only. Fee: adults, 50¢, children under 12, 10¢. Groups by reservation.

Fascinating collection of every type of wildlife, usual and unusual. Some early Americana now being collected for display. Ample parking.

From Rte. 4, north on Kinderkamack Rd. beyond Oradell. Large brown house, set back from road. Use long drive to parking area.

SECTION 2

Warren
Hunterdon
Somerset
Union

Warren County was a part of Sussex until 1824. Permanent settlers came into the area about 1725, but you can still see the old
mine holes of Dutch copper prospectors dating back to 1640,
and the famous Old Mine Road over which ore was hauled to the
coast. Legend has it that Tom Quick, the "Delaware Avenger,"
killed ninety-nine Lenni-Lenape Indians in Warren and neighboring Sussex in revenge for the murder of his father by Indians
whom he had befriended. Tom was never captured and was as
highly esteemed by the settlers as he was hated and feared by
the Indians.

Warren was named for Dr. Joseph Warren, a Revolutionary
hero who fell at Bunker Hill. The county's first Revolutionary
militia was led by William Maxwell, who later became a general commanding New Jersey's regular troops through much of
the war. The American Abolition Society was founded by a
Warren son, Benjamin Lundy, who first saw brutality toward
Virginia slaves in 1808 and never forgot or forgave the system
which made such treatment possible. It was therefore fitting that
Warren was among the first counties to furnish volunteers for
the Civil War; only three days after President Lincoln called
for men, Captain Earl Campbell of Belvidere showed up in
Trenton with a small force of men, much to the astonishment of
the unprepared authorities.

Warren is part of the Piedmont area, with a varied terrain
ranging from the Kittatinny Mountains and the Delaware Water
Gap to the rich farmlands around the Great Meadows, with its
many truck and dairy farms.

Hunterdon County, which dates back to 1713, once contained
nearly a fourth of the whole area of the state, but in 1738 Morris
County was carved out of it, and a century later Mercer County
was formed from its southern end. The first settlement in the

region was made by Quakers in 1676 at the falls of the Delaware north of Trenton.

The Revolutionary War touched Hunterdon principally at the ferries on the Delaware. Washington's army crossed the river at Coryell's Ferry (Lambertville) in his retreat from the British, and after the winter at Valley Forge it was there that he landed to begin his New Jersey campaign.

Three heroic officers of Hunterdon made the famous crossing of the Delaware possible by quietly collecting boats on the river, hiding them below Coryell's Ferry, and delivering them in time for the embarkment at McConkey's Ferry, now called Washington's Crossing.

There is an amusing hundred-year-old legend about the two towns of Hopewell and Amwell in Hunterdon. They were supposed to be the contractions used by the Stout family, whose members lived in the two nearby communities, and who used to greet each other with "Hope you're well," and "I am well." Actually, the names were brought from England by Quaker settlers.

Hunterdon's shoreline on the Delaware is almost thirty miles long, and beyond the river are rolling hills and beautiful valleys where dairy products, poultry, livestock, and fruit are produced.

The Rev. Theodorus J. Frelinghuysen, forebear of many state and national leaders, established the Dutch Reformed Church, in 1719, in Somerset County. His son John took over the ministry after his death and is regarded as the founder of Rutgers University (chartered as Queens College in 1766). In fact, Queens was in Somerset but the land on which it stands was ceded to Middlesex in 1850.

Washington spent the winter of 1778–79 at the Wallace House in Somerville, and wrote his Farewell Address to the Army while quartered at Rockingham, the home of the Widow Berrien, in Franklin Township in 1783.

Somerset was the home of the legendary Revolutionary spy, John Honeyman, who lived in Griggstown. The story goes that as a butcher delivering meat to the British he passed back and forth through their lines, spying out their strength and deployment, and that his reports paved the way for Washington's victory at Trenton. His house still stands in the old village on the banks of the Delaware and Raritan Canal, and his monument may be seen at Washington Crossing State Park.

Union County is the second smallest in area in the state, yet ranks third largest in industry. Its county seat, Elizabeth, is the second oldest in New Jersey. Early in the nineteenth century, when Newark and Elizabeth were in the same county, each town demanded that a new court house be built within its boundaries. The argument grew so heated that the Legislature ordered a popular election. At that time the laws did not specify the age or sex of a voter. In one of the hottest contests in New Jersey's history, the election took place in a carnival atmosphere. Women, children, and babies in arms all voted (several times); teenagers vied with each other to see who could cast the most votes in the shortest time; men and boys disguised themselves in women's clothing. The final tally, in favor of Newark, was so astonishing (Newark had cast as many votes as there were inhabitants aged one day to one hundred years), that the election was set aside and a new law passed limiting the voters to male adults. Newark won honestly the second time and woman suffrage had to wait more than a century before being restored.

Within the present Union County there were eighteen Revolutionary battles or skirmishes, fought in Elizabeth, Rahway, Westfield, Connecticut Farms (Union), and Springfield. British and Hessian troops under the German General Knyphausen were brought to a standstill by American forces at Connecticut Farms in June 1780, and when word came that Washington was back with reinforcements, retreated to Elizabeth. As they left the Farms, they set the village afire, burning down the church. One British soldier deliberately fired through an open window and killed Mrs. James Caldwell, wife of "the fighting parson." Sixteen days later, 5,000 British troops marched forth and met the American regulars and militia at Springfield. During the battle, the Americans ran out of wadding for their muskets. The Rev. Mr. Caldwell gathered up the Watts hymnals which had been saved from the burning church, and running to the soldiers as he tore out the pages, shouted, "Give 'em Watts, boys! Give 'em Watts!"

Bushkill Falls

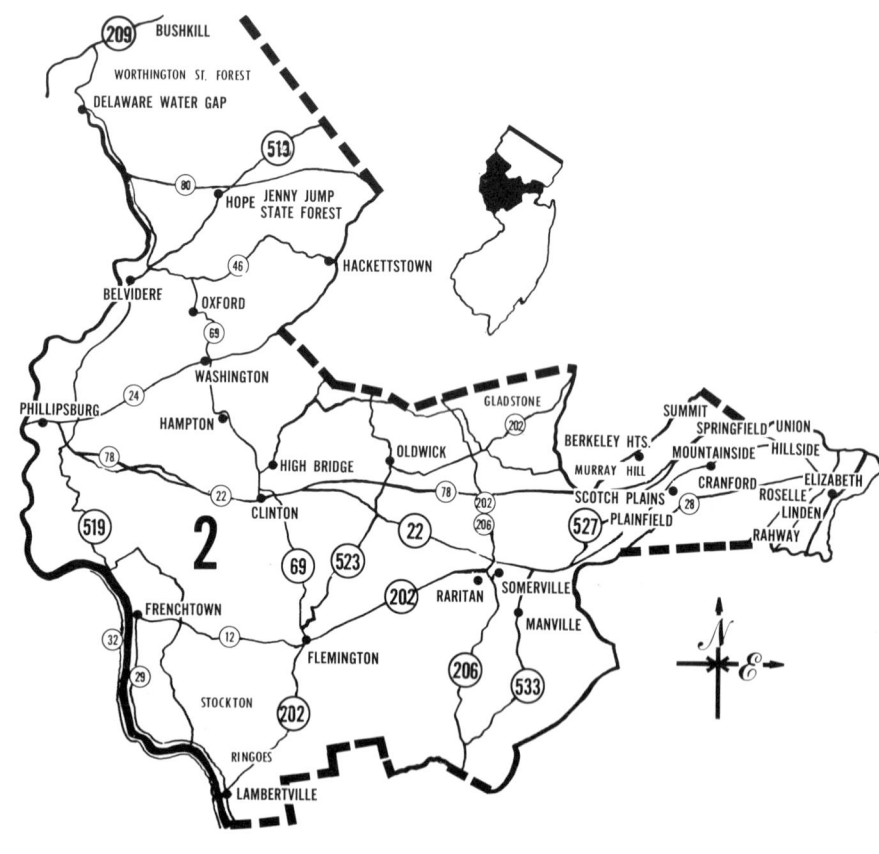

DELAWARE WATER GAP TRIP

A pleasant day trip for the whole family may be had by following Rte. 46 west to the Delaware and driving 15 miles farther into Pa. Beyond Hackettstown, one passes through the rich dairy and truck farmland of Great Meadows, along the Pequest River and through the Gap to Stroudsburg, Pa. Visit the Wild Animal Farm, then continue on to Bushkill Falls. Returning, for an interesting side trip, follow the east bank of the Delaware for a few miles. Leave Rte. 46 at Bridgeville, continue to Foul Rift, a dangerous rapids. Here the annual Delaware Down River Race for canoes and kayaks is held in early June. At nearby Oxford one may see the ruins of Oxford Furnace, first U.S. blast furnace, built in 1741. If time allows, consider visiting the State Fish Hatchery, Game Farm and Stephens State Park, all located off Rte. 46 in the Hackettstown area.

BUSHKILL FALLS

Bushkill, Pa.   Tel.: (717) 588-6634

Hours: daily, Apr. 1–Nov. 1, 8 a.m. to dusk. Entrance fee; group rates.

300 feet of waterfalls and gorges. Large picnic area with tables and fireplaces; children's playspace; boating; refreshment and gift stand.

Rte. 611 over bridge to Pa.; Rte. 402 to Marshall's Creek; then Rte. 209 to Bushkill.

POCONO WILD ANIMAL FARM

Rte. 611 Alternate, Foxtown Hill, Stroudsburg, Pa.   Tel.: (717) 421-7871

Hours: daily, May–Nov., 9–5:30. Entrance fee.

Wild animals; bison, elk, llamas, deer, monkeys, etc. Many roam free, may be petted and fed. Bottle milk for baby animals. Fire engine ride; picnic grounds, several outdoor grills available. Ice cream and soft drinks. Ample parking.

After Delaware River Bridge, take second ramp (U.S. 611 Alt., North). Or continue to Stroudsburg on Interstate 80, leave at Exit 191 south to 611 Alt. South.

STEPHENS STATE PARK AND SAXTON FALLS

Willow Grove–Waterloo Road, Hackettstown, N.J.   Tel.: (201) 852-2390

Hours: daily. Admission free.

Wooded park on Musconetcong River, with fireplaces, facilities for picnicking, fishing, baseball; children's playground. Dam, canal, swimming at Saxton Falls.

From Rte. 46, Hackettstown center; north 2 miles.

WORTHINGTON STATE FOREST

Columbia, N.J.   Tel.: (201) 231-9605

Fees: Picnic tables, 50¢; small boat landing, $1.00.

The tract has 4 miles of frontage on the Delaware River. Facilities include hunting, fishing, hiking, picnicking, camping. No bathing.

On Delaware River, 4 miles Northeast of Delaware Water Gap via Rte. 611.

STATE FISH HATCHERY

Grand Ave., Hackettstown, N.J.   Tel.: (201) 425-3676

Hours: daily, 8–4:30. Admission free. Tours: guides for groups available, apply: Hayford State Fish Hatchery, Hackettstown, N.J. 07840 or telephone.

Large hatchery with over 200 ponds; 3 hatchery buildings. Cold drinks only; picnic at Stephens State Park.

From Rte. 46, Hackettstown center; south 2 miles on Grand Ave.

STATE PHEASANT FARM

Hackettstown, N.J.   Tel.: (201) 425-3461

Hours: daily, 8–4:30. Admission free.

Farm area includes mostly pheasant and deer. No eating facilities; picnic at Stephens State Park.

From Rte. 46, Hackettstown center; south 4 miles on Grand Ave. past Hatchery.

MOUNT BETHEL SKI AREA

Mount Bethel Rd., between Port Murray and Hackettstown, N.J. Tel.: (201) 852-5340

Hours: Tues.–Sat., 7 P.M.–10:30 P.M.; Sat., 9:30 A.M.–10 P.M.; Sun., 9:30–7 P.M. Fees: vary.

Snow-making equipment. 3 tows; 3 trails; vertical drop 195 feet. Rentals; ski school: nights, weekends, holidays; clinic for high school, college programs. Snack bar; no nursery; no overnight lodging.

Mt. Bethel Road, off Rte. 46 (Warren County).

OLD MINE ROAD

Perhaps the oldest U.S. highway. Probably built by Dutch settlers about 1650. Road runs from Delaware Water Gap to Kingston, N.Y., about 100 miles. Served to bring copper ore from Kittatinny Mountains to the Hudson River. Still in generally good condition, it passes through wild, rugged country. Many old stone houses, farms, and cemeteries, especially in Sussex County.

From Blairstown, north to Millbrook. Turn either east or west.

Old Mine Road

JENNY JUMP STATE FOREST

Hope, N.J. Tel.: (201) 459-7366

Hours: daily. Fee for picnic tables.

High up on Jenny Jump Mountain, this Warren County forest provides beautiful views of the countryside and the Delaware Water Gap. Facilities include picnicking, nature study, hiking, hunting. Camping area; shelters available.

CAMP PAHAQUARRA COPPER MINE

Old Mine Rd., Pahaquarry Township, N.J.

Hours: write Camp Ranger, Camp Pahaquarra, Columbia, N.J. 07832. Admission free.

300-year-old copper mine. Original "mine hole" and 50 feet of gallery can be seen.

From Rte. 94, Blairstown; north to Millbrook through Hardwick Center; west 6 miles on Old Mine Rd.

VOORHEES STATE PARK
R.D. Glen Gardner, N.J. 08826   Tel.: (201) 638-6969

In the hills of Hunterdon County, this state park has scenic view of countryside; picnicking, camping and nature study.

Rte. 22 to Clinton, then 5 miles north via Rtes. 69 and 513.

NEW HAMPTON GENERAL STORE
R.F.D. Hampton, N.J. 08827   Tel.: (201) 537-2324

Hours: weekdays, 10–5; Sun., holidays, 12–5; closed all national holidays. Admission free.

One half general store, bazaar and emporium looks as it did a hundred years ago, with cracker barrel, pot-bellied stove, and vintage housewares. Other half sells items such as old-fashioned penny candies.

From Rte. 22 at Clinton, follow Rte. 31. Store halfway between Clinton and Washington.

SPRUCE RUN STATE PARK
c/o Voorhees State Park, Glen Gardner, N.J. 08826   Tel.: (201) 638-6969

This state park, located in Hunterdon County, is a reservoir with excellent fishing. Facilities include picnicking and bathing.

3 miles north of Clinton.

ROUND VALLEY STATE PARK
c/o Voorhees State Park, Glen Gardner, N.J. 08826   Tel.: (201) 638-6969

This 4,000-acre tract lies in the crater of Cushetunk Mountain. The reservoir is the second largest body of water in the state and offers fishing and boating. Facilities include campsites, bathing and picnicking.

South of Clinton; west of Rte. 31.

IORIO GLASS SHOP
Box 304, Flemington, N.J. 08822   Tel.: (609) 782-5311

Hours: weekdays, 9–5:30; Sun., 12–6. Admission free. Group tours by reservation.

Visitors may see glass being cut. Glass blowing demonstrations every Sat. and Sun. Also large display of early American, Jersey, Sandwich and Venetian glass and stemware.

Rte. 202, just south of Flemington traffic circle.

CLINTON HISTORICAL MUSEUM

Clinton, N.J. 08809

Hours: Apr. 1–Oct. 31, Tues.–Fri., 1–5; Sat., Sun., 10–5. Closed Monday. Fee: adults, 50¢; children to high school, 25¢; special group rates.

1763 mill, 1790 kitchen and weaver's shop, 19th-century carpenter's shop, harnessmaker's, 1875 little girl's room, glass case exhibit room. Dolomite limestone quarry; Deat's farm collection. 8-passenger Kayot-Clipper rides up Spruce Run River. Artisans every other weekend; collections every other week. 2-week concerts in amphitheatre; flea markets; arts and crafts.

On west side of dam. Rte. 22 to Rte. 78 to Clinton, Pittstown turnoff; turn right; at stop sign, turn right; on West Main St., bear left at Clinton House.

ADVENTURE HILL FARM

Highway 31 North, Clinton, N.J. 08809   Tel.: (201) 638-6676

Hours: by appointment only, minimum of six. Fees: $1.00; prekindergartners, free. Group rates: 75¢; chaperons, drivers, free. Tours: 1–1½ hours.

Especially suited for school trips. Private farm; tour includes educational talk on farm animals; large variety of animals: many may be petted; peacocks; migratory waterfowl; sheep; goats. Organic kitchen garden. Picnicking.

On Rte. 31 north of Rtes. 78 and 22, directly across from Spruce Run Reservoir.

FLEMINGTON AGRI-MARKET
84 Park Ave., Flemington, N.J. 08822   Tel.: (201) 782-4717
Hours: Mon. only, 9 A.M. on. Admission free.
Indoor livestock auction. Egg auction daily.
Rte. 202 to Flemington.

BLACK RIVER AND WESTERN RAILROAD (Steam)
P.O. Box 83, Ringoes, N.J. 08551   Tel.: (201) 782-6622
Hours: Mid-April–Oct.: Sat., Sun., major holidays; November: Sundays only. Schedule: Ringoes to Flemington, 10:45, 12:15, 1:45, 3:15, 4:45; Flemington to Ringoes: 11:30, 1:00, 2:30, 4:00, 5:30. Fees: Round trip, adults, $2; children (6–12), $1; One way, adults, $1; children, 50¢. Children under 5, free. Group rates: 25–100, adults, $1.75; children, 80¢; over 100, adults, $1.50; children, 75¢. Weekday trains available for groups by advance reservation.
Full-size restored equipment dating from 1875. Coaches equipped as they were before age of electricity and steam heat: pot-belly stoves, oil-burning lamps, etc. Oldest wooden "President's car" in use today. Ride is through scenic farm country. Rest rooms, snack bar, picnic facilities at Ringoes.
Flemington Depot: Turntable Junction, town center.
Ringoes Depot: west of Ringoes on Cty. Rte. 579, ¾ mile from junction of Rtes. 202 and 31.

MUSIC CIRCUS
Lambertville, N.J. 08530   Tel.: (609) 397-1500
Hours: Perf. Tues.–Fri. evenings, 8:40; Sat. evenings, 6 and 9:30; Sun., 7:30 P.M., June–Sept.
Theatre-in-the-round under a tent features Broadway musicals and stars. Excellent restaurants nearby.

CORYELL'S FERRY
Bridge St., Lambertville, N.J. 08530   Tel.: (609) 397-2336
Hours: every 30 minutes, 1 P.M.–dusk, mid-June–Labor Day. Fee. 30-minute trip.
Open-deck pontoon boats for the scenic trip up the Delaware, across to New Hope and back to Lambertville in a revival of ferry route in the Revolutionary period.
Rte. 202 to Lambertville. At bridge, bear left to ferry sign.

BULL'S ISLAND STATE PARK

R.D. 2, Stockton, N.J.   Tel.: (609) 397-2949

A 67-acre island on the Delaware River. Facilities include camping area, fireplaces, picnic tables, boating, fishing and nature area.

3 miles north of Stockton on Rte. 29.

PEAPACK SKI TOW, INC.

Gladstone, N.J.   Tel.: (201) 234-1356, 234-0942

Hours: weekdays, holidays except Christmas, 10 A.M.–4:15; night skiing, Mon.–Thurs., 7:45–10:15 P.M. Fees for admission, tows, night skiing.

1,000-foot slope. 5 trails, 1 jump. Instructions, rentals. For information regarding conditions, call:

> Bowcraft's Sport Center—(201) 233-0675
> Denville Sports Center—(201) 627-3030
> Ken Johnson sports—(201) 273-6545
> Ken Mills Sport Shop—(201) 539-0660

On Rte. 206, 1 mile north of junction of Rtes. 202 and 206.

MAGIC SHOP

Oldwick, N.J. 08858   Tel.: (201) 439-2330

Hours: daily except Sun., 10–1, 2–5. Admission free.

Children's toy shop in colonial-period house: unusual selection of music boxes, clocks, handicrafts. Bunnyland at Easter, Santa at Christmas. Run for the benefit of the Bonnie Brae Farm for Boys.

Rte. 22, westbound, to Rte. 517; Rte. 517 to Oldwick.

U.S. EQUESTRIAN TEAM HEADQUARTERS

Pottersville Rd., Gladstone, N.J. 07934   Tel.: (201) 234-0155

Hours: 10–1 daily except Sun. Open all year. Call in advance. Fee: contribution expected.

Here the horses and riders of the famous U.S. team are trained to represent our country in international equestrian events, particularly the Pan-American and Olympic Games. Occasional horse shows.

Off Rte. 22, at Somerville, travel north on Rte. 202-206 (which becomes 206). Turn left on Rte. 512 towards Pottersville.

OLD DUTCH PARSONAGE AND WALLACE HOUSE

Washington Place, Somerville, N.J. 08876 Tel.: (201) 735-1015

Hours: daily, except Mon., 10–12, 1–5; Sun., 2–5. Fee: adults, 25¢; children under 12, free. Tour: reservations by groups required.

Parsonage of Dutch colonial architecture, built 1751. Combine with visit to Washington's headquarters at Wallace House, across the street: a restored colonial home, which served as Washington's headquarters during winter of 1778–79. Same hours and fees.

Rte. 22 to Somerville center; follow signs.

SOMERSET COUNTY PARKS

DUKE ISLAND PARK

Off Old York Road, Raritan, N.J. Tel.: (201) 722-4118

Family, group picnicking. Boat pavilion, snacks, restrooms. Canoeing, rowboating in canal; fishing; protected ice skating (natural ice). Playground. Nature trail, wildflower trail. Summer concert series and performing arts. Admission free.

From Rte. 22, Somerville Circle, south on Rte. 206; turn right on Somerset St.; through Raritan; Somerset St. becomes Old York Road.

GREEN KNOLL GOLF COURSE

Off Garretson Rd., Bridgewater Twp., N.J. Tel.: (201) 722-1300

Fees: call clubhouse.

Regulation championship layout. Tourneys; industrial league activity. Pro shop, snack bar. Winters: sledding, skiing but no ski facilities.

GREEN KNOLL TENNIS CENTER

At Green Knoll Golf Course

Hours, fees: call Somerset County Park Commission (201) 722-1200

10 courts; 5 for night play. Pro shop. Paid instruction programs; free clinics.

From Rte. 22, north on Country Club Rd. to Garretson Rd.; right on Garretson Rd.

COLONIAL PARK

Mettlers Rd., Franklin Twp. (Somerset), N.J.

Family, group picnicking; playgrounds; fishing. Nature walk. Animal display. Paddle-boat rentals (summer); public canoe launching ramp. 12-acre lake. 4 all-weather tennis courts.

SPOOKY BROOK GOLF COURSE

In Colonial Park. Tel.: (201) 844-7961

18-hole championship layout. Pro shop; snack bar.

From Rte. 22, Finderne Ave. exit; Finderne Ave. through Manville to Amwell Rd., left on Amwell Rd.

LORD STIRLING PARK

Off Maple Ave., Bernards Twp., N.J. Tel.: (201) 766-5955

Hours, fees: telephone for information.

Public riding stable. Instruction. Hayrides.

Rte. 287 north to No. Maple Ave. exit; No. Maple Ave. through Basking Ridge to South Maple Ave.

ROCKINGHAM

Rte. 518, Rocky Hill, N.J. Tel.: (609) 921-8835

Hours: Tues.–Sat., 10–12, 1–5; Sun., 2–5. Fee: adults, 25¢; children under 12, free. Reservations for groups required.

State-owned house (also known as the Berrien House) used by General Washington as headquarters from August to November, 1783, while the Continental Congress was in session at Princeton. Here Washington wrote his Farewell Address to the Armies. Authentic furnishings of the period.

Rte. 27 north from Princeton, left on Rte. 518 at Kingston.

Washington's Study, Rockingham

THE MODEL RAILROAD CLUB, INC.

94 Oakwood Dr., Murray Hill, N.J. 07971 Tel.: (201) 464-5315

Hours: Tues., Fri., 8–11 P.M., except holidays. Phone in advance: club alternates between periods of construction and operation. Admission free.

Model of the Lackawanna R.R. built by Club. Timetable operatic n like real railroad; telephone head-set communication.

F om Summit center, Mountain Ave. to traffic light at Bell Labs; ri ,ht on South then right on Oakwood Dr.

UNION COUNTY PARKS

ASH BROOK GOLF COURSE AND RESERVATION

Raritan Road, Scotch Plains, N.J.

Hours: open all year, weather permitting.

18-hole golf course. Also, 9-hole pitch-and-putt course.

WATCHUNG RESERVATION

Coles Ave. & New Providence Rd., Mountainside, N.J.

Hours: daily. Admission free.

Natural woodlands: hiking; observation tower; village circa 1840; picnicking, fireplaces. Watchung Stables: 55 horses; bridle trails. Surprise Lake: fishing; boating and boat rentals. Refreshment stand: weekends year round; daily, June–Aug.

Trailside Nature and Science Center

Tel.: (201) 232-5930

Hours: Sept.–June, weekdays except Fri., 3–5; weekends, holidays, 1–5. July–Aug., daily, except Fri., 1–5. Admission free. Tour: guides by appointment only.

In the Watchung Reservation, the center contains flora and fauna exhibits; mineral displays; live and mounted animals. Nature program: Sundays at 2 P.M. Five miles of nature trails.

Trailside Planetarium

Hours: Wed., 8 P.M; Sun., 3 and 4 P.M. Children under 8 not admitted. Admission free.

Facilities can accommodate only 35 persons at one time: tickets issued on first-come basis, on day of show, at Trailside office.

From Rte. 22, westbound; pass Mountainside center; right at New Providence Rd. traffic light. Follow signs.

CEDARBROOK PARK

Randolph Rd., Plainfield, N.J.   Tel.: (201) 756-2220

Hours: daily; iris display, May–mid-June. Admission free.

One of the largest public iris gardens in the U.S.; Shakespeare Garden with flowers mentioned in his works and those popular in his time: dogwood, daffodils, peonies, etc. Playgrounds, shuffleboard, tennis, baseball fields, field hockey, football, soccer, softball; fishing; ice skating; picnicking.

From Rte. 22 take Somerset St. Exit, Park Ave. to Randolph Road (about 2 miles).

WARINANCO PARK

St. Georges Ave., Roselle, N.J.

Hours: daily. Admission free.

This Union County Park has facilities for picnics, tennis, ball fields, ice skating (artificial ice rink). Lake for boating, fishing (rentals). In season: Japanese cherry trees, azaleas. Henry S. Chatfield Memorial Garden: tulips, annual plantings.

From Elizabeth center, south on Rahway Ave. Rahway Ave. becomes St. Georges Ave.

GALLOPING HILL GOLF COURSE AND PARK

Kenilworth Blvd., Kenilworth, N.J.

Union County Park offers 27-hole course; nine-hole pitch-and-putt course lighted for night play.

Ski Center

Located at #3 fairway of the single 9-hole course. 675-foot tow rope. Night skiing. Artificial snow. Equipment rental. Fees: Weekdays: 10–5, $2.00; 2–5, $1.00; 7–10, $2.00. Sat., Sun., holidays: 10–3; $3.00; 2–5, $2.00; 7–10, $3.00.

Exit 138, Garden State Parkway; west to Kenilworth.

BOWCRAFT'S SPORT SHOP AND PLAYLAND

U.S. 22, Scotch Plains, N.J.   Tel.: (201) 233-0675

Hours: daily, weather permitting, May–Oct., 10 A.M.–11 P.M. Admission free. Fees for activities.

Miniature golf; Go-Karts; archery; batting; driving range; electric U-Drive boats; pony, horse rides; table tennis. Snack bar. Arcade games; skee ball.

Rte. 22 westbound, past Westfield. Shop on right.

SCOTCH PLAINS TOUR

There are at least 30 pre-Revolutionary houses, and numerous others built before 1820. Except for the Inn, these are private residences, not open to the public, but are worthwhile walking or driving past. A descriptive brochure, prepared by the Junior Women's Club can be bought at the Public Library, Bartle St.

The Old Baptist Parsonage
347 Park Avenue

Osborn Patterson House
711 Westfield Road

DeCamp House
Old Raritan Road

Frazee-Lee House
11 Black Birch Road

"The Well"
1451 Rahway Road

Stage House Village and Inn
Park Avenue

Restaurant, antique and gift shops.

CANNON BALL HOUSE

126 Morris Ave., Springfield, N.J. 07081

Hours: Sun., 3–5; also by appointment: call Springfield Public Library, (201) 376-4930. Admission free.

Farmstead and dwelling, built mid-18th century. Now headquarters for and maintained by the Springfield Historical Society. One of the four houses which escaped burning by the British during the Battle of Springfield, June 23, 1780. The British were forced to retreat after the battle which marked the last time the enemy set foot on New Jersey soil. Exhibit of early American and Revolutionary War relics.

FIRST PRESBYTERIAN CHURCH

Church Mall and Morris Ave., Springfield, N.J. 07081   Church Office: 37 Church Mall.

Hours: daily. Admission free.

Present church built 1791 on site of original burned by British during battle of Springfield, 1780. Note adjacent Minute Man statue. It stands in the smallest N.J. State Park.

On Rte. 24, Springfield center.

First Presbyterian Church, Springfield

WASHINGTON ROCK STATE FOREST

Green Brook, N.J.

This 36-acre park is situated on a vantage point on the First Watchung Mountain. Here George Washington watched the movement of British troops during the Revolution. Picnicking facilities.

Off Rte. 22, west of Dunellen.

DRAKE HOUSE MUSEUM

602 West Front St., Plainfield, N.J.   Tel.: (201) 757-5320

Hours: Mon., Wed., Sat., 2–5. Admission free.

House built 1746, restored by Junior League of Plainfield, Historical Society and D.A.R. Rooms decorated in different period styles, from Colonial to Victorian. Changing exhibits.

From Rte. 22, Plainfield: exit on Somerset St. to Front St., turn right.

CRANFORD HISTORICAL SOCIETY MUSEUM
124 North Union Ave., Cranford, N.J. 07016   Tel.: (201) 276-0082

Hours: Sat., 10–12; Sun., 3–5. Tours: weekdays by appointment. Admission free.

Museum, erected circa 1840, is registered in the Library of Congress; contains memorabilia, documents, etc., of Township of Cranford. Outstanding photographs of buildings, people, events.

CRANFORD BOAT AND CANOE CO.
Springfield and Orange Aves., Cranford, N.J. 07016   Tel.: (201) 272-6991

Hours: daily, 11–11; Memorial Day–Labor Day. Hourly fee.

Canoes rented for trips on winding stream. Younger children must be accompanied by parent; age 12 and over may go alone. "Take-away" canoes; weekend rentals.

From Rte. 22 south on Springfield Ave., at Cranford-Westfield exit.

ESSO RESEARCH CENTER
Rte. 1 and Park Ave., Linden, N.J.   Tel.: (201) 925-1600

Hours: by reservation only; write Esso Research & Refining Co., Public Relations, P.O. Box 172, Linden, N.J. 07036. Tours: high school juniors and seniors, college preparatory students, science clubs, teachers.

Scientists at work creating new materials from petroleum and chemicals. Engine laboratories with highly sophisticated equipment for research on control of automotive pollution. Opportunity to learn about industrial research, its nature, environment and career opportunities.

Use main entrance on Linden Ave.

ELIZABETH CITY MARKET (Farmers' Market)
High St., Elizabeth, N.J.

Hours: Tues., Thurs., Sat., 8–3. Admission free.

3 block, open air market area. Farmers hawk plants, vegetables, fruit, etc. Meat, fish, drygoods in colorful displays. Interesting whether you buy or not.

From Rte. 1, Elizabeth center; east on Elizabeth Ave. towards Elizabethport. Market at right; Harmonia Bank, just beyond.

GENERAL MOTORS ASSEMBLY PLANT

1016 Edgar Rd., Linden, N.J. 07036   Tel.: (201) 486-6700

Hours: Mon.–Fri., 1:30 and 7:15 P.M. when plant is in production. No fee. Tour: groups of 10 or more, by appointment; 75 min.

Assembly plant for Cadillac and Oldsmobile. Interesting, informative to youngsters from age 8 up. No eating facilities.

On Rte. 1, opposite Linden Airport.

BOXWOOD HALL (BOUDINOT MANSION)

1073 East Jersey St., Elizabeth, N.J. 07201   Tel.: (201) 352-3559

Hours: weekdays except Mon., 10–12, 1–5; Sun., 2–5. Fee: adults, 25¢; children under 12, free. Tour: reservations for groups required.

Georgian-style house, with furnishings and paintings of 1750 period. The home of Elias Boudinot, President of Continental Congress, active in Revolution, and signer of Peace Treaty. Famous guests included Washington, Lafayette, and Hamilton.

SECTION 3

Middlesex
Mercer
Monmouth

Middlesex is one of the original four counties of East Jersey, created in 1675. A few years later John Inian built his ferry to cross the Raritan at what is now New Brunswick, and an inn for stopping over and changing horses on the road between New York and Philadelphia. A century or so after this, Commodore Vanderbilt ran a ferry from this point to New York. With the coming of railroads in the nineteenth century and super highways in the twentieth, Middlesex has grown as a connecting bridge between the two great cities.

While Washington was retreating from the British in 1776, his troops camped on the grounds of Queens College (now Rutgers). After the Battle of Monmouth in 1778, his troops were again in New Brunswick and General Washington allowed them to celebrate Independence Day with fireworks.

Today Middlesex is a farming and light industry county with a steadily increasing population. Old Queens, one of two Colonial colleges in New Jersey (the other being Princeton: New Jersey was the only colony to have two colleges), has grown into a great state university. It includes the Agricultural College where soil research led to the discovery of streptomycin and neomycin.

Mercer County was the scene of two famous battles of the Revolution: on December 25, 1776, Washington crossed the Deleware at McConkey's Ferry and recaptured Trenton, then marched ten miles north to Princeton to defeat the troops of Lord Cornwallis. The Continental Congress met at Princeton in 1783, convening in the college's Nassau Hall.

Captain William Bainbridge, who was born in Princeton, fought the Tripoli pirates in 1800. Later he commanded the *USS Constitution* which defeated the British frigate *Java* in the War of 1812. Another Princetonian who was at Tripoli was Robert Field Stockton. In 1812, he was a member of an expedition which explored the coast of Africa for the American Colonization Society, seeking land for the resettlement of freed American slaves. The site chosen became the colony and in 1847 the independent Republic of Liberia, first of the free republics of Africa.

Morven, the Governor's mansion, was originally one of the Stockton residences in Princeton. Former Governor Walter E. Edge, whose home it had been for a number of years, gave it to the state in 1944.

Monmouth County was the home of two of New Jersey's legendary heroines. Penelope Van Princis Stout's story has come down in several versions. One is that she was among the victims of the first recorded shipwreck off Sandy Hook in 1620. She and her ill husband were among the few who could get to shore. The sick man could go no farther, and the other passengers panicked and left the young couple to fend for themselves. Somehow, wet through and freezing, they lived for several hours, only to be attacked and scalped by Indians, who left them for dead. Penelope's husband was indeed dead, and her left shoulder was smashed (she never regained the use of her arm), and her abdomen was so badly torn that her intestines hung out. But she somehow managed to climb into a hollow tree, where she remained for several days in the extreme cold, with nothing to eat but bark and frozen tree gum. At last she was discovered by two Indians, one of whom wanted to kill her. But for some reason the other Indian insisted on taking her to the Indian camp, where she recovered and lived for a time with her captors. Finally she was returned to her own people in New Amsterdam, where she met and married Richard Stout. They settled at Shrewsbury, where they brought up ten children. When this incredible woman died at the age of 110, she left more than five hundred living descendents. The Stout family, now numbered in the thousands, still holds reunions in the county.

Washington's famous Battle of Monmouth gives us the story of another New Jersey heroine known as Molly Pitcher. Her real name was Mary Hays, and like many soldiers' wives of the time, she followed her husband with the Army, cooking and washing. During the battle, which was on a very hot day, more soldiers were collapsing from thirst than from enemy bullets. Mary repeatedly carried water to them from a nearby spring until her husband fell wounded beside his cannon. She took over the firing and remained on the battlefield until the British retreated.

The citizens of Monmouth erected a well on the battle site as a memorial, and there is also a plaque on the Monmouth Battle Monument, showing Molly in action at a cannon.

Modern Monmouth is a farming county, retaining much of its pre-Revolutionary character. Its coastline is made up of wonderful long stretches of sandy beaches. A summer visitor can walk through the past in the well-preserved homes and churches of Freehold and Englishtown, take a swim at any one of numerous beaches, and on the way home stop at a roadside truck garden to collect the delicious vegetables and fruit of the region.

4-H horse show at Thompson Park, Middlesex County. *Thomas J. Pollock*

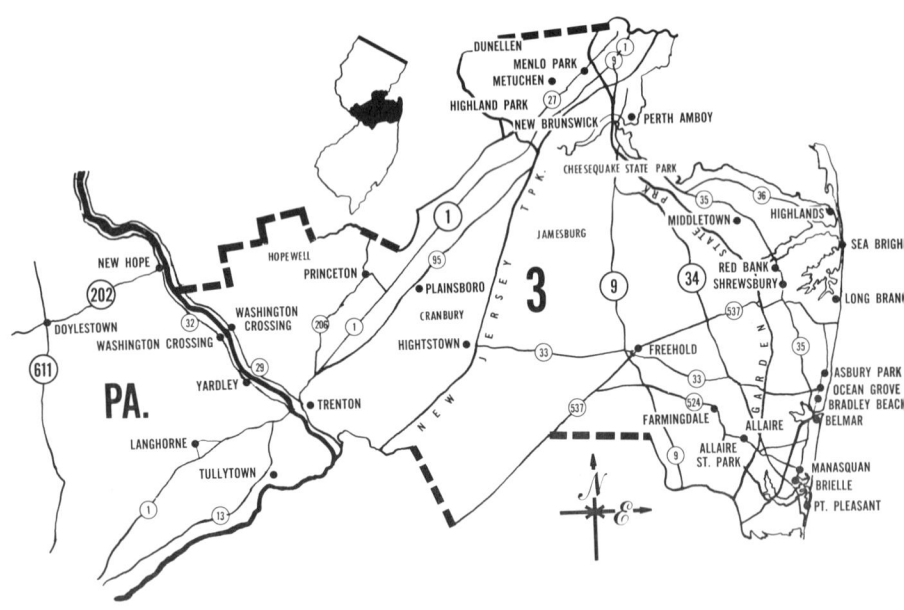

DUNELLEN
MENLO PARK
METUCHEN
HIGHLAND PARK
NEW BRUNSWICK
PERTH AMBOY

CHEESEQUAKE STATE PARK

JAMESBURG

MIDDLETOWN
HIGHLANDS
SEA BRIGH

RED BANK
SHREWSBURY
LONG BRAN

HOPEWELL
PRINCETON

PLAINSBORO
CRANBURY

HIGHTSTOWN

NEW HOPE
202
DOYLESTOWN
WASHINGTON
CROSSING
WASHINGTON CROSSING
611
PA.
YARDLEY
TRENTON
LANGHORNE
TULLYTOWN

3
9
34
537

FREEHOLD

ASBURY PARK
OCEAN GROVE
BRADLEY BEACH
BELMAR

524
FARMINGDALE
ALLAIRE
MANASQUAN
BRIELLE
PT. PLEASANT

ALLAIRE
ST. PARK

NEW JERSEY TPK.

GARDEN STATE PKWY.

N
E

NEW HOPE, PENNSYLVANIA

During the summer months the village of New Hope has something for everyone and every age. You can have a quiet or an active time, depending upon what you want. Wander down the streets, in and out of handicraft shops, art galleries, gift and souvenir shops, clothing and house furnishing stores. There are good restaurants and plenty of small eating and snack places. You can take a canal trip on a mule-drawn barge, hear a concert at the open-air Sun Dance, attend a professionally mounted play. You can go early and stay late. It's a crowded village during the summer but it provides an entertaining and unusual outing. For those interested in history, points of interest are: The Parry Barn and Parry Mansion on South Main Street; the Revolutionary War cannon on South Main and Ferry Streets; the Flood House with its handsome grillwork and lovely proportions.

The Barge Lock

On Canal from New Street.

Hours: May–Sept.; Wed., Sat., Sun. 1-hour trip. For private trips and large groups, reservation necessary. Fee.

Mule-drawn barges on the old Delaware Canal for private parties, large groups by reservation.

Bucks County Playhouse (State Theater of Pennsylvania)

Tel.: (215) 862-2041

Hours: May–Sept., weekday evenings; matinees, Wed. and Sat. at 2. Schedule, rates write Bucks County Playhouse, New Hope, Pa.

Housed in the old Parry grist mill, beside the Delaware River. Professional casts, Broadway productions.

On South Main Street.

THE MERCER MUSEUM OF EARLY AMERICAN LIVING

Pine and Ashland Streets, Doylestown, Pa. 18901 (Bucks County)
Tel.: (215) 348-4373

Hours: Mar.–Dec., Tues.–Sat., 10–5; Sundays, April–Oct. only, 1–5; closed Jan., Feb. Fees: adults, $1.00; students, 50¢; special rates for families, groups. Groups by appointment only.

The famous Mercer Museum holds the country's richest collection of early American daily life artifacts, from settlement to the time of mass production. Tools and products of 40 crafts and pre-steampower industry on display.

From New Hope, Rte. 202 west to Ashland St.; Ashland St. to Pine St.; turn left.

RALPH STOVER STATE PARK

Point Pleasant, Pa.   Tel.: (215) 297-5090

Admission free.

Park with fireplaces, picnic tables; refreshment stand; lake with good swimming and bathhouses; fishing. Cabin rentals: first Sunday after Memorial Day through last Saturday before Labor Day for Pennsylvania residents. Nonresident rental periods, April 14 to first Saturday after Memorial Day, and Tuesday following Labor Day to December 20. Apply in advance to Park Foreman.

From Rte. 32, north.

FONTHILL MUSEUM AND MERCER TILEWORKS

East Court St., Doylestown, Pa.

Hours: daily, 10–3. Fee: contribution.

House of German medieval architecture; interior set with tile from all over the world. One ceiling depicts the voyage of Columbus. Adjoins Mercer Tileworks.

WASHINGTON CROSSING STATE PARK
(New Jersey)

Washington Crossing, N.J.

Hours: daylight. Park admission free. Fee for admission to McKonkey's Ferry Museum.

Park commemorates Washington's famous crossing of the Delaware River on Christmas night, 1776, before the Battle of Trenton. An open-air theater and the State Forest Nursery are in the park. McKonkey's Ferry Museum, built 1737, restored as colonial inn and museum. The Flag Museum is in McKonkey's Barn. Picnic facilities for families and organized groups.

WASHINGTON CROSSING STATE PARK
(Pennsylvania)
Washington Crossing, Pa.

Admission free.

Across the Delaware from its N.J. counterpart. Many picnic areas. Obtain fire permit from guards. Points of special interest include:

LOWER PARK

Washington Crossing Memorial Building
Hours: weekdays, 11–5; Sun., 12–5.

Famous painting "Washington Crossing the Delaware," on loan from the Metropolitan Museum of Art. Narration with music every half hour. Library of the American Revolution in east wing.

Point of Embarkation
Site of the crossing on Christmas night, 1776. The attack launched here marked the turning point of the Revolution.

Old Ferry Inn
Present structure superimposed on the original building; adjacent to the Ferry which played a significant part in Washington's crossing of the Delaware.

Taylor House
Hours: 8:30–5; Sat., 8:30–11:30.

Built in 1812 by Mahlon K. Taylor, now headquarters for the Park Commission.

Lagoon
Near western entrance; a bird sanctuary. During winter months it is used for ice skating.

UPPER PARK

Bowman's Hill Tower
Monument marks spot where Continental troops spied on Hessians in nearby Trenton. Pine forests and wildflower preserves surround tower which may be climbed for a fine view.

Turn north on River Rd. after crossing bridge.

Wildflower Preserve
Tel.: (215) 862-2924

100-acre preserve of native Pennsylvania flowers, trees, shrubs, ferns. Appointments for guided tours at Preserve headquarters.

Thompson-Neely "House of Decision"
Tel.: (215) 862-2915

Hours: weekdays, 10–5; Sun., 1–5.

Oldest section of this beautiful house built in 1702. Served as headquarters during encampment in 1776 for Lord Stirling, Capt. James Moore and Lt. James Monroe, later President of the United States. Furnished with period pieces.

Old Mill
Where miller Thompson ground grain for Washington's starving army.

Nature Education Center
Tel.: (215) 862-2921

Hours: Mar. 1–Nov. 1, 4 P.M.; Nov. 2–Feb. 28, 3 P.M.; children's program, Mar. 1–Nov. 1.

Bird-banding programs.

BELLE MOUNTAIN SKI AREA

Valley Road, Hopewell, N.J. 08230   Tel.: (609) 392-1089; snow phone, (609) 392-1089

Hours: daily, 10–4:30, 5:30–10; weekends, holidays, 10–4:30. Fees: vary for residents, nonresidents, day and evening, weekends, holidays.

Snow-making equipment; 1 lift; 3 tows; 5 trails from expert to junior; vertical drop 190 feet. No rentals; clinic; no base lodge; snack bar in trailer; no nursery.

Off Rte. 29 (River Rd.) on Valley Road.

FALLSINGTON

Fallsington, Pa.

Several buildings of colonial interest, including two historic Friends' meeting houses.

From Rte. 1 westbound; turn south at Tyburn Rd., 3 miles from Morrisville, Pa.

PENNSBURY MANOR HOUSE OF WILLIAM PENN

Tullytown, Pa.   Tel.: (215) 946-0400

Hours: daylight-saving months: 8:30–5 daily, 1–5 Sun.; standard-time months: 9–4:30 daily, 1–4:30 Sun. Fee: over 12, 50¢; no charge for school groups; adult group rate (10 or more), 35¢. Tours: for school groups only, by reservation.

Colonial manor house recreated in 1683 period with appropriate furnishings. Houses largest collection of 17th-century furniture in state of Pennsylvania. Outbuildings include ice house, bake and brew house, caretaker's office, smokehouse, blacksmith shop, sheep shed. Farm animals to pet. A replica of William Penn's barge at river's edge. No eating facilities.

From Rte. 1 westbound; turn south on Rte. 13, beyond Morrisville.

TRENTON

Visitors to the capital city of New Jersey may wish to add some of the following points of interest to their tour of the State House. All are easily reached from State Street, the main thoroughfare of Trenton.

New Jersey State House

Trenton Cultural Center

Hours: see individual listings. For guided tours through complex: School Reservation Service, New Jersey State Museum, Cultural Center, Trenton, N.J. 08625 Tel.: (609)292-6347

State House

121 W. State Street

Houses state court system.

Calder sculpture, State Museum

State Museum

205 W. State Street

Hours: Museum, Auditorium, Mon.–Sat., 9–5; Sun., 2–5; Planetarium demonstrations, 2, 3, 4 P.M. every Sat., Sun., holiday. For program information, call (609) 292-6464. Museum closed Christmas, New Year's, Thanksgiving days.

Changing exhibits in fine and decorative arts and cultural history in Museum; permanent exhibits in science, history; school programs in art, science and history by reservation. Planetarium offers weekend programs open to public and school programs by reservation. Auditorium schedules school programs as well as weekend programs open to public. All programs free.

The State House from the Delaware River

State Library
185 W. State Street

Hours: see text. No charge for programs.

Family groups: film programs on Sat., Sun., State holidays, 3 and 4 P.M., Archives Exhibit Room. School groups: lecture-demonstrations (1-hour long) on New Jersey history or government. Reservations required; minimum 22 students, maximum 44. For library clubs, 6th graders and older, tours of the Library may be arranged; reservation required; 1½ hours long. Lecture and library club programs given Monday through Friday whenever staff and facilities permit.

Battle Monument

At terminus of Broad and Warren Streets.

Hours: weekdays except Mon., 10–12, 1–5; Sun., 2–5. Fee: adults, 25¢; children under 12, free. Tours: reservations for groups required. School classes admitted free when accompanied by teacher.

Monument commemorates Battle of Trenton. For view of city, use 155-foot elevator to observatory.

North on Broad St., one mile from War Memorial.

The Old Barracks

South Willow St.   Tel.: (609) 394-5692

Hours: weekdays, June–Aug., 10–5; Sept.–May, 10–4; Sundays, June–Aug., 2–5; Sept.–May, 1–4. Fee: adults, 75¢; children to 12, 25¢; students, 50¢; maximum $2.00 for family groups.

Finest colonial barracks in U.S., built 1758–59. Housed British, Hessian, and Continental troops during Revolution. Collections of pre-1800 artifacts: currency, pottery, firearms, etc.

One block north of War Memorial.

The Trent House

593 South Warren St.   Tel.: (609) 695-5939

Hours: May–Aug., weekdays 10–5, Sun., 1–5; Sept.–Apr., weekdays 10–4, Sun., 1–4. Fee: adults, 25¢; children, 10¢. Groups by reservation.

Built in 1719 by Justice William Trent who named and planned the city. Colonial furnishings and beautiful gardens.

From State St. south on Willow St. to John Fitch Way, then to Bridge St.; left on Bridge to Warren St., north to Trent House.

Cadwalader Park

Parkside Ave.

Hours: park open daily; lunch stand, kiddie rides during summer only. Admission free; small charge for rides.

Recreation area containing picnic grounds; concert bandstands; playing fields; tennis and lawn bowling facilities, etc.; plus small indoor and outdoor zoos. Beautiful rose garden containing over 50 varieties; duck pond with cherry trees; "Swamp Angel," the Civil War cannon.

From Rte. 1, westbound; take Parkside Ave. Exit.

PRINCETON UNIVERSITY

Orange Key Guide Service, Stanhope Hall, Princeton, N.J. Tel.: (609) 452-3603

Hours: year round, Mon.–Sat., 9–5; Sun., 2–5 (except Christmas Day, Thanksgiving Day). Tour: with or without guide. Groups must reserve in advance.

The beautiful 2300-acre campus of the nation's fourth oldest university, chartered in 1746, may be seen all year at no charge. Many good places to eat are within walking distance of the campus and one may picnic at nearby Carnegie Lake, or in the surrounding open countryside. Buildings of special interest below:

Nassau Hall

Built in 1756, still in use as University administrative offices. Headquarters of Continental Congress, 1783.

Princeton University Chapel

Third largest university chapel in the world, with especially fine stained glass windows. Open daily until midnight.

Firestone Library

Hours: library open all year; gallery hours: Mon.–Sat., 9–5; Sun., 2–5; restricted hours during vacations and on holidays.

Contains papers of Woodrow Wilson and John Foster Dulles.

Art Museum

Hours: Tues.–Sat., 10–4; Sun., 2–4; closed Mondays and principal holidays.

One of the most comprehensive university museums. Collections are richest in the art of early Mediterranean civilizations, Western Europe, the United States, and East Asia.

Museum of Natural History

Hours: Mon.–Sat., 9–5; Sun., 2–5; closed principal holidays.

Collections of fossil plants, minerals, vertebrates, etc., and a reconstructed dinosaur. Housed in Guyot Hall.

McCarter Theatre of Princeton University

University Place   Tel.: (609) 921-8700

Hours: Oct.–May; Box Office, 10–5. Special matinees for school groups. Prices vary. Season subscription discounts. School and group discounts. Reservations accepted by phone.

Professional drama and special events such as ballet, films, modern and classical concerts. Famous for annual Triangle Show by undergraduates. To join mailing list write: McCarter Theatre, P.O. Box 526, Princeton, N.J. 08540.

Rte. 1 to Washington Rd. exit; west to Nassau St.; turn left; from Nassau, left turn on University Place.

BAINBRIDGE HOUSE

158 Nassau Street, Princeton, N.J. 08540   Tel.: (609) 921-6748 & 921-6817

Hours: Daily 10–3, Sat. 1–3, Sun. 2–4. Admission free. Advance notice required for groups.

Bainbridge House, built in 1766 for Job Stockton and birthplace of Commodore William Bainbridge, is the headquarters of the Historical Society of Princeton. The house is partially restored, and two rooms have been furnished with period furniture.

MORVEN (Governor's Residence)

Stockton St., Princeton, N.J.

Georgian-style mansion, built 1701. Revolutionary period furnishings and portraits, beautiful gardens. The house is not open to the public, but may be seen from the street while touring Princeton.

Morven, the New Jersey Governor's residence

DAVID SARNOFF LIBRARY

RCA-David Sarnoff Research Center, Princeton, N.J. Tel.: (609) 452-2700, Ext. 3004

Hours: Mon.–Fri., 10–3. Admission free. Tours: advance reservations for groups larger than 6. School groups: suggested for 8th grade and up.

Personal collection of books, documents, correspondence, memorabilia assembled by General Sarnoff for over 6 decades. Auditoriums equipped to take groups as large as 300. Lectures and slides geared to particular interests.

From Rte. 1, south on Hightstown Road 0.3 mile; left into Fairview Ave., proceed into RCA grounds; follow signs to left to Library.

JOHNSTON HISTORICAL MUSEUM
National Headquarters, Boy Scouts of America, Rte. 1, New Brunswick, N.J. Tel.: CH 9-6000

Hours: Mon.–Sat., 9–5; Sun., 1–5. Admission free. Tour: one hour inside; one-half hour outside.

Small museum devoted to Scouting. Numerous visitor-operated exhibits, including a weather station and a short-wave radio unit. Outdoor conservation and nature exhibits.

From N.J. Turnpike; New Brunswick Exit. Museum just beyond junction of Rte. 1 and Rte. 130.

THE SPERRY AND HUTCHINSON CO.
Rte. 27 and Vineyard Rd., Metuchen, N.J. 08840 Tel.: (201) 287-1500

Hours: 9–12, 2–4. Suitable for 7th grade through college; adults. Tour information: Consumer Relations Dept., Rte. 22 and Cramer Ave., Green Brook, N.J. 08812.

This cash discount business was started in 1896, incorporated in 1900. Trading stamps remain its most important business. Unusual storage procedure, packing, shipping and distribution of the varied merchandise.

At intersection of Rte. 27 and Rte. 287.

CRANBURY HISTORICAL AND PRESERVATION SOCIETY MUSEUM

So. Main Street, Cranbury, N.J. Tel.: (609) 395-0657

Hours: Tues., Fri., 2–5, April–Nov.; closed winter months. Group tours by appointment. Admission free.

Small museum with rooms furnished to depict Cranbury history to pre-Civil War era. Furniture; artifacts; costumes; farm machinery, etc.

Behind Cranbury Inn.

Bedroom in Cranbury Historical Society Museum

FIRST PRESBYTERIAN CHURCH

So. Main Street, Cranbury, N.J.

Hours: daily. Groups by appointment.

Excellent example of church architecture of its time: built 1743. Cemetery beside church has stones dating back to pre-Revolutionary times when the village was a stagecoach stop.

Opposite Cranbury Inn.

The Rutgers Coat of Arms

Old Queens, erected in 1809, the first permanent building at Rutgers

RUTGERS UNIVERSITY, THE STATE UNIVERSITY OF NEW JERSEY

Rutgers, the 8th Colonial college, was founded in 1766 under royal charter from George III. Originally called Queens College, the name was changed in 1825. Over the years it became the land grant college and the state university of New Jersey. Rutgers' three campuses—at New Brunswick, Newark, and Camden—include colleges of arts and sciences, engineering, agriculture, law, pharmacy, and nursing, a number of graduate schools, an evening college, research bureaus, and a women's division, Douglass College. Enrollment of degree candidates exceeds 35,000.

College of Agriculture and Environmental Science
Nichol Avenue. Tel.: (201) 247-1766

Visitors are always welcome to the College Farm, although there are no planned tours. Sheep and dairy barns, poultry and pig farms, and the display gardens, with their extensive plantings of native shrubs and trees, are accessible to the public seven days a week, including holidays. Field days and special public events announced in advance in most of the state's newspapers.

From Rte. 1, south of New Brunswick traffic circle, enter College Farm on Ryders Lane in either direction: east to horticultural farms, west to college buildings and animal farms; or enter from Nichol Ave. in New Brunswick.

Frank G. Helyar Woods Nature Trail
Horticultural Farm No. 1 near intersection of U.S. Route 1 and Ryders Lane.

A trail about ⅔ mile long winds in a circle through the woods, with stops that show features of particular interest. Walking time about 45 minutes.

Geology Museum
Geology Hall, Queens Campus, College Ave. and Somerset St., New Brunswick. Tel.: (201) 247-1766, ask for Geology Dept.

Hours: daily, 9–4; Sat., 9–2; call or write in advance. Tour: class groups welcomed; arrange in advance.

Mineral displays, featuring those found in New Jersey; also a mummy and a Mastodon skeleton.

University Art Gallery

Voorhees Hall, Hamilton St. Tel.: (201) 247-1766

Hours: Sept.–June, Mon.–Sat., 9:30–4:30, Sun., 1:30–4:30; Wed. eve., 6:30–9; July–Aug., closed weekends. Also closed during University holidays. Admission free. Tours: by arrangement only; call Ext. 6237; limit, 50 persons; school groups: suitable for grade school up.

Changing exhibits. Yearly graphics sale. Historical exhibits. Contemporary artists' work often for sale. Catalogue of Rutgers Collection, $1.00.

William L. Hutcheson Memorial Forest

Amwell Road, ½ mile east of East Millstone.

Free guided tours for ten or more persons may be arranged with Forest Director, Department of Botany, Rutgers University.

EDISON PARK MEMORIAL TOWER AND MUSEUM

Rte. 27, Menlo Park, N.J. Tel.: (201) 549-3299

Hours: Tues.–Sat., 10–12, 1–5; Sun., 12–5; closed Monday. Fee: adults, 25¢; children under 12, free. Tour: reservations for groups required.

Museum contains model of Edison's laboratory. Tower topped by huge light bulb marks spot where first incandescent bulb was made.

From Garden State Parkway, Exit 131; Rte. 27 southbound. Tower on right, one mile from Parkway.

MILLSTONE FORGE

Millstone Forge Association, Inc., North River St., Millstone, N.J. Tel.: evenings, (201) 369-4590

Hours: Sundays, 2–4, May, June, Sept., Oct., Nov. Other days by appointment. Fee: contribution.

Shop interior has open forge, large bellows; 2 horn anvils, beakhorn anvil. Equipment dating from 18th century; some mechanical equipment from early 1900's. Collection of wheelwright tools.

From New Brunswick center: west on Hamilton St. which becomes Amwell Rd. (Rte. 514); cross bridge over Millstone River, turn right on River Rd. at bridge. Shop is next to Mill at The Forge Studio.

Hickman Hall, Douglass College

Rutgers Art Gallery

MIDDLESEX COUNTY PARKS

JOHNSON PARK

River Road, Highland Park–Piscataway, N.J. Tel.: (201) 247-2567

Hours: daily until dusk. Admission free. Group affairs by reservation.

Facilities: ball fields, picnic area and fireplaces; wildlife preserve, bird sanctuary; race track for shows, trotting; historical blacksmith shop; tennis; golf driving; playgrounds; ice skating; fishing. Special Events: horse shows; antique show; Freeholders Tennis Tournament; dog shows; art show.

From N.J. Turnpike, New Brunswick exit (#9) to Rte. 18 west; follow signs to Highland Park; first left after crossing bridge into Highland Park.

Harness racing at Johnson Park. *National Free Lance Photographers Assn., Inc.*

DONALDSON PARK

Riverview Ave., Highland Park, N.J. Tel.: (201) 247-2567

Hours: daily until dusk. Admission free; group affairs by reservation.

Facilities: ball fields; picnic area with fireplaces; tennis; boat launching; golf driving; playground.

From N.J. Turnpike Exit 9, Rte. 18 West; follow signs to Highland Park; right on 2nd Ave. South (4 blocks after crossing bridge).

MERRILL PARK

Middlesex-Essex Turnpike, Woodbridge, N.J. Tel.: (201) 247-2567

Hours: daily. Admission free; groups by reservation.

Facilities: ball fields; picnic area with fireplaces; playground; tennis; animal shelter; day camping; ice skating.

East on Green Street in Woodbridge from Rte. 27.

RARITAN ARSENAL GOLF COURSE

Woodbridge Ave., Edison, N.J. Tel.: (201) 548-8654

Hours: daily, 7–dusk. Greens fees: weekdays, county residents, $2.50; nonresidents, $3.00; Sat., Sun., holidays: county residents, $3.50; nonresidents, $4.50; weekday special: senior citizens, Middlesex County College, and people under 18, $1.00.

9 holes, 2,691 feet; pro shop; snack center. Special events include Annual Freeholders Tournament, Annual Junior Golf Tournament, Senior Citizen Tournament.

From N.J. Turnpike, Exit 10, Interstate Rte. 287 to Woodbridge Ave. South, 2 miles; from U.S. Rte. 1, east on Old Post Road, Edison, for ¼ mile, then right on Mill Road. Follow signs.

ROOSEVELT PARK

U.S. Rte. 1, Edison, N.J. Tel.: (201) 247-2567

Hours: daily until dusk. Admission free; group affairs by reservation.

Facilities: ball fields; picnic area with fireplaces; tennis; stadium with track; playground; golf driving; day and overnight organized camping; outdoor theater; ice skating; fishing.

Garden State Parkway, Exit 130; Rte. 1 south 1 mile.

TAMARACK GOLF COURSE

Hardenburg Lane, East Brunswick, N.J. Tel.: (201) 821-8881

Hours: Daily, 7–dusk. Greens fees: weekdays, county residents, $3.00; nonresidents, $5.00; Sat., Sun., holidays: county residents, $5.00; nonresidents, $8.00. Reservations required Sat., Sun., and holidays; fee, 25¢ per player.

18 holes: 6,993 feet for championship play, 6,303 for regular play, 5,844 for women; practice range; clubhouse.

Rte. 130 to Washington Place, No. Brunswick; east to Hoey's Corner Road–Hardenburg Lane.

Restored forge at Thompson Park. *Will Gainfort*

THOMPSON PARK

Perrineville Road–Gatzmer St., Jamesburg (Monroe Township), N.J.   Tel.: (201) 247-2567

Hours: daily until dusk. Admission free; skiing entrance fee. Group affairs by reservation.

Facilities: ball fields; picnic area with fireplaces; tennis; playground; day and overnight group camping; animal shelter; radio-controlled model airplane flying; horse show rings; golf driving; swimming; boating; ice skating; fishing; skiing. Special Events: horse shows; 4th of July fireworks; Boy, Girl Scout Jamborees.

Ski Village

P.O. Box 1341, Nixon, N.J. 08817   Tel.: (201) 521-1150
Hours: daily, 10:30–4:30, 5:30–10 P.M. Fees: county residents, $1.50; nonresidents, $2.50.

Free sledding. Snow-making equipment. 2 rope tows; 1800-foot trail; vertical drop 135 feet. Rentals; instructor; lighted night skiing. Sledding hours same as for skiing. Log cabin lodge; snack bar.

From N.J. Turnpike, Exit 8A; left on Forsgate Drive to Jamesburg; right on Perrineville Rd.–Gatzmer Ave.

BUCCLEUCH MANSION

Buccleuch Park, Easton Ave., New Brunswick, N.J.

Hours: Sun., 3–5, Memorial Day–Labor Day. Admission free. Tour: school groups only; weekdays, by reservation.

House built 1734. Sabre scars; secret stairway; original French wallpaper in halls. Picnic area and playground in adjacent park.

From New Brunswick center, Easton Ave. to park; turn right; then left at bandstand.

ARROWHEAD SKI AREA

YMCA, Marlboro, N.J. 07746   Tel.: (201) 946-4598

Hours: daily, 1–5, 6:30–10:30; weekends, holidays, 9–5, 6:30–10:30 (no evening hours, Sundays). Fees: vary with members, non-members, days, etc.

Snow-making equipment; 3 tows; 3 trails with machine snow; 2 beginners' slopes with natural snow only; vertical drop of 100 feet. Rentals; John Canova Ski School (Nov.–Mar.); clinic. No overnight lodging. Food vending machines; no nursery.

Opposite State Hospital, Rte. 520.

CHEESEQUAKE STATE PARK

Matawan, N.J.   Tel.: (201) 566-2161

Hours: daily. Fees: entrance, parking.

Within a heavily industrialized area, this lovely park offers forest-like surroundings. Facilities: bathing, picnicking, fishing, camping and hiking. Of particular interest to those with an interest in botany: abundant variety of flora.

6 miles southeast of Perth Amboy; Garden State Parkway Exit 120.

MONMOUTH COUNTY HISTORICAL ASSOCIATION

70 Court St., Freehold, N.J. 07728   Tel.: (201) 462-1466

Hours: weekdays except Mon., 11–5; Sun., 2–5. Library open 2nd and 4th Saturdays, 11–5. Admission free. Groups by appointment. Building closed: July 15–31 and Dec. 15–31.

Georgian-style building; exhibits of furniture and decorations of Colonial and Revolutionary times arranged in period rooms. Collection includes displays of silver, china, historic paintings; primitives depicting early scenes and people. Also contains flag and sword captured during the Battle of Monmouth as well as "Washington at Monmouth," painted by Emanuel Leutze. The Library contains a collection of early maps and manuscripts including the Monmouth Patent of 1665; complete file of county newspapers; large genealogical and reference library. Third floor devoted to interests of school children: early Indian relics, Colonial and Revolutionary items, miniature furniture, guns, dolls, toys, costumes, local wild life, crafts.

From Garden State Parkway, Exit 123 onto Rte. 9 South. From Exit 100A onto Rte. 33 west. Court St. runs northwest off Main St.

FREEHOLD TOUR

After visiting the Monmouth County Historical Association to see relics and reminders of the Battle of Monmouth, the Revolutionary War, and the early settlers, a tour toward Englishtown might be of interest. Include visits to Old Tennent Church, St. Peter's Church, and the Monmouth Battleground.

Old Tennent Church

Main St., Tennent, N.J.

Hours: Sun. service only; visitors welcome to view grounds and interior from doorway. Admission free.

Very old glass in windows. Erected 1751, housed wounded after Battle of Monmouth. Small collection of battle relics. Old cemetery in churchyard.

From Main St., Freehold, west on Throckmorton St., to Tennent St.

St. Peter's Church

Throckmorton St., near Main St., Freehold, N.J.

Hours: open daily, visitors welcome. Admission free.

Building ante-dates Revolution. During Battle of Monmouth, church was main hospital of British until retreat.

From Main St., Freehold, north on Throckmorton St.

Monmouth Battleground

Englishtown Rd., Freehold, N.J.

Marker indicates area where Gen. Washington routed the British and turned the tide of the war. Proposed site for Federal reclamation as an historical site.

Old Tennent Church

Headquarters, Monmouth County Historical Association

ALLEN HOUSE

Sycamore Ave., Shrewsbury, N.J. 07701

Hours: call Monmouth County Historical Association, (201) 462-1466.

House built in 17th century, in process of restoration.

Rte. 35 to Shrewsbury.

CLINTON'S HEADQUARTERS

150 W. Main St., Freehold, N.J. 07728

Hours: call Monmouth County Historical Association, (201) 462-1466.

Built circa 1706, a fine example of pre-Revolutionary craftsmanship currently being restored by the Historical Association. Headquarters of Gen. Clinton before the Battle of Monmouth.

MARINE PARK

Wharf Ave., Red Bank, N.J.

Admission free.

Area on Navesink River for family recreation, includes boat basin, tennis courts, shuffleboard courts, picnic area. From the car one may see races and regattas, skating, ice-boating, and in the summer, listen to band concerts.

South on Rte. 35, across Cooper's Bridge. Riverside Ave. to Wharf Ave.

Marlpit Hall

MARLPIT HALL

137 King's Highway, Middletown, N.J. 07748   Tel.: (201) 671-3237

Hours: Tues., Thurs., Sat., 11–5; Sun., 2–5. Closed January. Admission free. Groups by appointment.

Dutch Colonial building erected in 1684 with addition circa 1712, owned by the Monmouth County Historical Association. Furnished in period style; example of early county culture.

From Garden State Parkway Exit 117. South on Rte. 35 to Middletown; right on King's Highway.

GARDEN STATE ARTS CENTER

Telegraph Hill Park, Holmdel, N.J.   Tel.: (201) 264-8600

Hours: mid-June–mid-Sept.; check local newspaper for events, hours, fees.

The Center features professionally mounted concerts, plays, musicals, ballets, and other cultural events. It sponsors special free events for schools, grades 1–12, in spring and fall. There are special free programs during the day, summers, for disadvantaged children in the state. In cooperation with the Jaycees, it holds a state-wide talent contest: preliminaries after school closing and finals in Sept.; 8 categories; applications through high school music departments.

At Exit 116 on the Parkway: no other entrance.

HOLMES-HENDRICKSON HOUSE

Longstreet Road, Holmdel, N.J. 07733   Tel.: (201) 462-1466

Hours: Tues., Thurs., 1–5, May–Oct. For other times, and for groups, appointment necessary.

14-room Dutch Colonial house built circa 1717. Furnishings of 17th and early 18th centuries. Presented by the New Jersey Bell Laboratories to the Historical Association.

Note: To borrow the 16mm film (sound and color) "A Home in Our Heritage," about this house, call 811 (N.J. Bell Telephone Business Office).

Next to the Monmouth County Park in Holmdel.

SHREWSBURY TOUR

The churches of Shrewsbury will provide guides for large groups by prearrangement. Only the following are regularly open:

Presbyterian Church at Shrewsbury

Sycamore Ave., Shrewsbury, N.J. Tel.: (201) 747-3557

First building erected in 1727; present building dated 1821. Burial ground.

Friends' Meeting House

Broad St. and Sycamore Ave., Shrewsbury, N.J.

Hours: by reservation only. Admission free.

Quaker house of worship, built 1816.

Old Christ Church

Broad St. and Sycamore Ave., Shrewsbury, N.J. Tel.: (201) 741-2220

Hours: daily. Admission free.

Established 1702, present structure built 1769. Original grant from King George II. Spire one of two in country with a British crown. Interior features carved eagle on pedestal and one of 8 extant copies of "Vinegar Bible," printed 1717.

From Garden State Parkway at Red Bank; left on Rte. 520 to Rte. 35; south to Shrewsbury.

ALLAIRE STATE PARK AND THE DESERTED VILLAGE OF ALLAIRE

Box 218, Farmingdale, N.J.   Tel.: (201) 938-2371

Hours: daily, 9–5, June–Sept.; closed Mon., Sept.–June and Thanksgiving; Dec., Jan., and Feb., open Sat., Sun. only. Park grounds open all year. Fees: entrance, parking; fees for horse and carriage rental; train rides (Sat., Sun., holidays, May–Nov.).

Park features picnic areas, fireplaces, grills, tables, playground; bridle trail; fishing; hiking, nature study; camping.

Deserted Village was a self-contained community, center of a bog-iron industry. Blacksmith shop, charcoal house, grist mill, and saw mill. Museum once a bakery. Blast furnace; church; carpenter shop; work-manager's cottage; foreman's cottage; farm buildings include carriage house and stables (now a riding academy). General store serves snacks; souvenirs. Narrow gauge, old-time railroad rides.

12 miles southeast of Freehold via Rtes. 9 and 524. 3 miles west of Garden State Parkway from Exit 96 (southbound) or Exit 97A (northbound).

TWIN LIGHTS
Rte. 36, Highlands, N.J.

Hours: grounds open daily. Admission free.

Old twin lighthouse, once marked entrance to New York Bay. Hilltop area with unequalled view, being restored as marine museum. Parking lot; picnic tables; telescopes.

Note: For beautiful drive along the Atlantic Highlands, turn left on Ocean Drive, marked "Scenic Route." Rejoins Rte. 36.

From Garden State Parkway; Exit 117, east on Rte. 36 to Twin Lights.

MONMOUTH COUNTY SHORE RESORTS
The following towns have beach facilities for nonresidents; fee for parking and bathhouses. All have good accommodations for overnight or longer, restaurants, amusement areas, access to summer theatres, public golf courses, fishing, boating, etc. For information write Chamber of Commerce or Borough Clerk.

All resorts accessible from Garden State Parkway or Rte. 35.

Asbury Park
Outstanding beach; over a mile of boardwalk with varied amusements; fresh- and salt-water pools; fishing from pier, party boat, or charter boat. For complete details visit Asbury Park Official Resort Bureau, Boardwalk, or write: Dep't 4, Convention Hall.

Belmar
Boardwalk amusements and beach, pool or river swimming. Two fishing piers and marina.

Bradley Beach
Beach and pool swimming; boardwalk amusements; band concerts; dances.

Brielle
Noted fishing center on Manasquan River; boats of all types available.

Long Branch
World's largest fishing pier, bathing, boardwalk.

Manasquan
Beach, boardwalk, and amusements.

Ocean Grove
Beach and pool swimming, boardwalk, summer concerts.

Sea Bright
River and ocean beaches; fishing.

LEONARDO MARINA
Leonard Ave. off Rte. 36, Leonardo, N.J.

State-operated marina on Sandy Hook Bay: 6-foot draft; 198 berths; accommodates 65-foot lengths.

SANDY HOOK STATE PARK
Highlands, N.J.   Tel.: (201) 872-0115

Hours: daily. Fees: for parking, bathing, bathhouse.

Park occupies southern portion of the barrier peninsula of Sandy Hook. Facilities: bathing, bathhouse, picnicking, fishing service, tour service through nature area. No picnic tables; picnic fires not permitted. Noted for Spermaceti Cove area and holly forest.

SECTION 4

Burlington
Ocean

Burlington is the largest county in area in New Jersey. Its famous pine barrens, a wilderness of scrub forest, extend into neighboring Ocean County, but most of its ground is enormously fertile, producing a large proportion of the vegetables of the Garden State.

No major battles were fought in Burlington County during the Revolution, but its people were the victims of many British raids.

Fishing at Seaside Heights

In 1778 a British force came up the Mullica River to Batsto to punish the "Jersey Pirates," as they called the privateers who harassed British shipping, and to destroy the iron works which were furnishing cannon for the Continental Armies. But fifty ironworkers made such a good stand that the British, believing they were facing Colonial regulars, retreated.

Burlington was the birthplace of Captain James Lawrence. He was fatally wounded aboard his ship the *Chesapeake* during a battle of the War of 1812. As he lay dying he issued the famous order, "Don't give up the ship!" which became the watchword of the American Navy.

Bordentown, settled by Quakers in 1682, had many famous residents, among them Joseph Bonaparte, brother of the French Emperor, who lived there from 1816 to 1839. Clara Barton, who later founded the American Red Cross, came to Bordentown to teach in 1851. Unhappy at the lack of education for poor children, she started New Jersey's first public school in a one-room building. A few years later the townspeople insisted that her work be supervised by a male principal, and she resigned.

Some of the early settlers of Ocean County were whalers who had a station at Long Beach. Little Egg Harbor and Tuckerton (then called Clamtown) were the center of American privateer activity against the British blockade during the Revolution. In 1782, when the war was drawing to a close, angry Tories and English soldiers burned the settlement at Toms River. In retaliation, a young English prisoner, Lt. Charles Asgill, was chosen by lot to die. Feeling ran so high against the killing of an innocent young man that some months later he was released and became the hero of the hour. His release did a great deal to restore good feeling between former enemies.

Today dairy, truck, and poultry farming, commercial fishing, and resorts are the primary activities in Ocean County. Its miles of wide beaches, sport fishing, and protected bays attract over two million summer visitors annually.

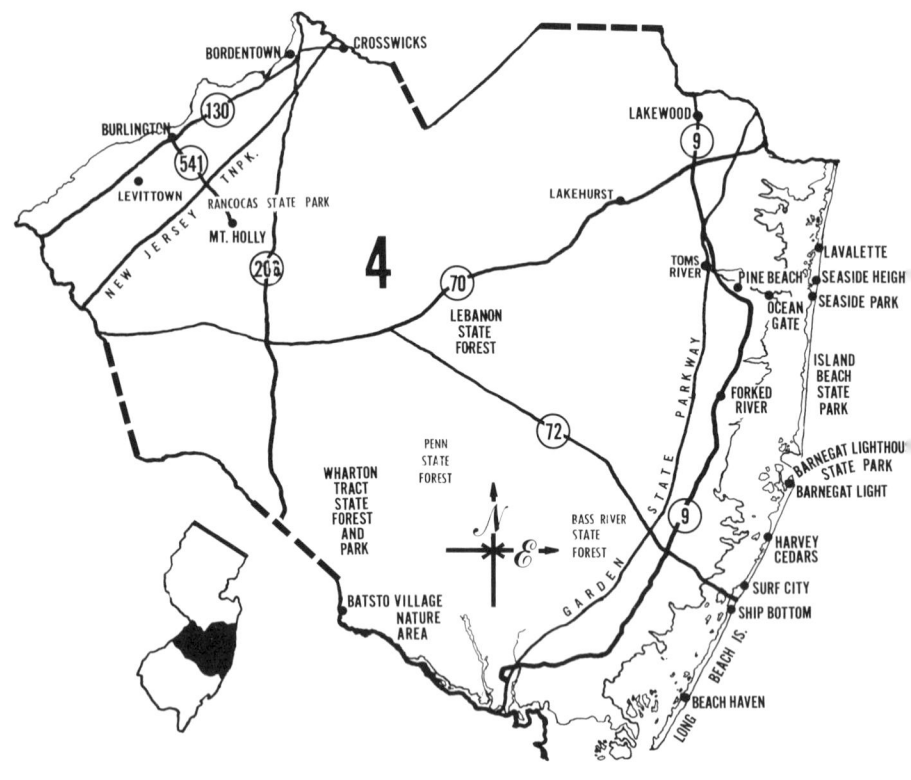

BORDENTOWN AND CROSSWICKS TOUR

2 historic towns with many old buildings still standing. Most of these are private residences, open to the public during Open House Day, held annually in May. Descriptions of these and others which can be entered appear below. Bordentown Chamber of Commerce will send, on request, the pamphlet "A Walking Tour of Bordentown."

Clara Barton Schoolhouse

Crosswicks and Burlington Sts., Bordentown, N.J.

Hours: by reservation only; write Bordentown Historical Society, or phone (609) 290-0014. Admission free.

First free public school in the state, established 1852 by Clara Barton, founder of American Red Cross. Fully restored.

From Rte. 206, west on Crosswicks St., left on Burlington St.

Gilder House

Crosswicks St., Bordentown, N.J.

Hours: daily. Admission free.

House with Revolutionary period pieces donated or lent by local families; some from the Point Breeze estate once occupied by Joseph Bonaparte, brother of Napoleon. Adjacent Carslake Community Center has picnic tables, outdoor grills and stadium, free. Large groups by reservation only; call (609) 298-3769.

From Rte. 130 southbound; right on Crosswicks St. after intersection with Rte. 206.

Private Residences
(not usually open but worth driving by)

Francis Hopkinson House

101 Farnsworth Ave.

Fine Colonial house, built 1750 by merchant John Imlay; home of Francis Hopkinson, a signer of the Declaration of Independence.

Joseph Hopkinson House

Bordentown Military Institute Campus

Home of author of "Hail, Columbia," son of Francis Hopkinson.

Hoagland's Tavern

Historic hotel and tavern, sacked by Hessian troops before the Battle of Trenton, 1776. Fine iron grillwork balcony.

Friends' Meeting House and School

Rte. 130, Crosswicks, N.J.

Hours: by reservation only; phone (609) 298-2772. Admission free.

Quaker Meeting House, built 1773 to replace earlier log structure dating from 1692. Interior is of cedar with hand-wrought nails and has cast-iron stove made at Atsion. Revolutionary cannonball imbedded in wall. Building has been in use every Sunday since its completion. Adjacent schoolhouse existed before public school system.

From Rte. 130, southbound; east after intersection with Rte. 206.

BURLINGTON–MT. HOLLY TOUR

Most of the old buildings in these neighboring towns can be seen in a few hours' time. There is a park in Burlington, on West Federal Street, for picnicking and relaxation.

Burlington, the provincial capital of West Jersey, was settled in 1677 by Quakers. They came from London and Yorkshire and evidently desired to keep their origins distinct: they divided the town down High Street with Yorkshiremen on the east side up to Trenton and Londoners on the west side down to Camden.

BURLINGTON COUNTY HISTORICAL SOCIETY

James Fenimore Cooper House

457 High Street, Burlington, N.J. 08016   Tel.: (609) 386-4773
Hours: Sun., 3–5; other days by reservation. Admission free.

This 18th-century house, birthplace of the first American novelist, contains the complete writings of Cooper as well as relics and records of the town's early history.

Pearson-How House

Next to Cooper House.   Tel.: (609) 386-4773
Hours: Sun., 3–5. Tours at other times by reservation.

Built about 1705 as English frame house; enlarged about 1725. Unusually large for the period and beautifully proportioned. In process of being furnished in early 18th-century antiques: has a Pearson clock, made in the building, circa 1710; Chippendale side chair from the Penn family; Windsor chair belonged to Gov. Bloomfield.

Della Biddle Pugh Library

Behind Pearson-How House and Cooper House.

Genealogy and history collected by the Society; tools and antiques of Colonial period. Manuscript collection open to researchers by appointment.

Aline Wolcott Museum

Behind Pearson-How House and Cooper House.

Original copy of Isaac Collin's Bible. Samples of Nathaniel Coleman's famous silverware. Unusual Lithopane from France; jimrickshaw, a sample of those made in town and sold all over the world, including Japan and China. Wolcott collection of lamps, lighting fixtures dating from 2000 B.C. to 1928.

Old Friends' Meeting House and Burial Ground

High St., Burlington, N.J.

Hours: by appointment. Admission free.

Original building erected 1784 has much of the original wood-work, glass, and fittings.

Old St. Mary's Church

West Broad and Wood Sts., Burlington, N.J. 08016

Hours: by appointment, call (609) 386-0902. Admission free.

Oldest Episcopal Church in New Jersey, built in 1703, during reign of Queen Anne, whose gift of a silver communion service is still in use. "New" St. Mary's nearby was designed by Richard Upjohn and begun in 1846. In the old churchyard are buried many early leaders of New Jersey: Gov. Bloomfield, Elias Boudinot, Col. Daniel Cox (1st Grand Master of the N.J. Masons).

Old St. Mary's Church

New St. Mary's, designed by Richard Upjohn

Capt. James Lawrence House

459 High St., Burlington, N.J.   Tel.: (609) 386-4815

Hours: Tues.–Sat., 10–12, 1–5; Sun., 2–5. Admission free.

Capt. James Lawrence, the celebrated naval hero, was born here in 1781. His dying order, "Don't give up the ship!" is the motto of the U.S. Navy.

South on Rte. 130 to High Street; turn right.

The following are private residences and not open to the public. However they are well worth looking at:

Boudinot House

West Broad Street, Burlington, N.J.

Residence of Elias Boudinot, President of the Continental Congress, 1804–1821.

Shippen House

Talbot St. and Riverbank, Burlington, N.J.

Built in 1750, this beautiful house was the summer home of the Shippen family. Peggy Shippen married Benedict Arnold.

St. Mary's Hall

Riverbank, Burlington, N.J.

Founded in 1837 as Episcopal school for girls by Bishop Doane, composer of hymn "Fling Out the Banner! Let It Float."

Wood Street, Burlington, N.J.

The street is worth a leisurely tour; numerous beautiful old homes. Of special note:

Revell House

Oldest house in Burlington County.

Grant House

Where Gen. Grant was staying when he received the announcement of President Lincoln's assassination.

John Woolman Memorial

99 Branch St., Mount Holly, N.J.   Tel.: (609) AM 7-3226

Hours: weekdays, 9–6; Sun., 1–6. Admission free; groups by appointment only.

Simple 18th-century house, built 1783 on property of John Woolman, famous Quaker. Contains period furniture and memorabilia.

From N.J. Turnpike, southbound, Exit 5; then about 2 miles east on Rte. 541 to Mount Holly.

County Court House

High St., Mount Holly, N.J.

Hours: Mon.–Fri., 9–4:30. Admission free.

A fine example of colonial architecture, built 1796.

The Old School

Brainerd St., Mount Holly, N.J.

Hours: Mon.–Fri., 9–4:30. Admission free.

Restored nineteenth-century schoolhouse.

RANCOCAS STATE PARK

Excellent boating in both North and South Branches of Rancocas Creek. Good area for nature study.

Off Rte. 537, north of Masonville.

LEBANON STATE FOREST AND PASKIM POND

New Lisbon, N.J. Tel.: (609) 894-2740

Hours: daily. Fees: entrance, parking, motorless boats.

Fine hunting. Facilities include bathing, boating and fishing, hiking, picnic area. Camping sites; cabins available on shore of Paskim Pond.

17 miles southwest of Lakehurst off Rte. 70; 30 miles east of Camden on Rte. 72.

PENN STATE FOREST AND LAKE OSWEGO

c/o Bass River State Forest, New Gretna, N.J. 08224 Tel.: (609) 296-2554

Hours: Daily. Fees for picnic tables, motorless boats.

In the heart of the Pine Belt section; sweeping view of forest from Bear Swamp Hill. Lake Oswego, developed from a cranberry bog reservoir, offers bathing, picnicking, hiking, boating and fishing. Fine hunting in forest.

McGUIRE AIR FORCE BASE

New Jersey 08641 Tel.: (609) 724-2100

Hours: open only through appointment; Mon.–Sat. Tours: limited to groups of 50. Write: Wing Information Office, 438 Military Airlift Wing, McGuire Air Force Base, N.J. 08641; give size of group, ages, preferred dates.

Tour includes passenger terminal; flight line fire station; when available, walk through one of base's planes.

WHARTON STATE FOREST

Batsto, R.D. 1, Hammonton, N.J. 08037 Tel.: (609) 561-0024

New Jersey's largest state forest located in the pine area. The forest abounds in rare plants, native fish, and game. Historically the center of South Jersey's once thriving iron industry, it reached its peak of production during the Revolution and the War of 1812. It provides limited facilities for bathing, camping, picnicking. Canoe trips can be taken through the wilderness area.

Batsto Village

Hours: daily, 10–6, Memorial Day–Labor Day; winter months, 11–5. Fee for tour. Buildings may be entered only with guide.

Village produced munitions for Continental Army. Contains iron furnaces; Mansion House with 80-foot tower; grist mill; carriage house; blacksmith shop; snacks.

Batsto Nature Area

Hours: daily.

2 miles of footpaths adjoining the Village. Identification of plants and shrubs native to the region. Picnicking.

For guide service for groups, write, Wharton Forest Office.

From Garden State Parkway, Exit 50 or 52; then Rte. 542 to Batsto.

Batsto Mansion, in Batsto Village, Wharton State Forest

BASS RIVER STATE FOREST AND LAKE ABSEGAMI
New Gretna, N.J. 08224   Tel.: (609) 296-2554

Hours: daily, May 30–Labor Day; Sat., Sun., May 1–30, and Labor Day–Oct. 31. Fees for entrance, parking, motorless boats.

Oldest state forest with long established forest plantations of several interesting species. Facilities: bathing, picnicking, hiking, nature study, hunting, fishing and boating. Lake Absegami offers bathing, cabins, campsites and camp shelters.

6 miles west of Tuckerton, via Garden State Parkway Exit 50 or 52.

OCEAN COUNTY PARKS
Ocean County Park
Lakewood, N.J.

Hours: daily. Admission free.

Picnic area in pine grove; patrolled lake for swimming; athletic field; horse-drawn wagon rides.

From Garden State Parkway, Exit 91.

Lake Pohatcong
Tuckerton, N.J.

Hours: daily. Admission free.

Bathing and picnic facilities at a cedar lake.

Lake Manahawkin
Ocean County Park

Facilities for bathing and picnicking.

Intersection of Rtes. 9 and 72.

FRIENDS' MEETING HOUSE
Off Main St., Tuckerton, N.J.

Hours: by reservation only. Admission free.

Society of Friends founded in Tuckerton in 1702. Present building built in 1708 to replace smaller early one.

PULASKI MONUMENT
Radio Rd., Tuckerton, N.J.

Commemorates the massacre of part of the Revolutionary forces under Brigadier General Pulaski while attempting to repulse the British invasion of the Mullica Valley.

STATE GAME FARM (Pheasant)

Forked River, N.J.   Tel.: (609) 693-3081

Hours: daily, Mar.–Sept. recommended. Admission free. Tour: guides available; suitable for school groups.

On pre-arranged tour, guide explains game bird raising, incubation, hatching process, etc. No lunch facilities nearby.

From Garden State Parkway, east on Rte. 9. Turn left at Forked River; signs on stone pillars mark entrance on right.

ISLAND BEACH STATE PARK

Seaside Park, N.J. 08752   Tel.: (201) 793-0506

Hours: daily. Fees: entrance, parking, bathing; additional fees for fishing area.

10-mile stretch of sand dunes. Area divided into a botanical zone, wildlife sanctuary, and recreation area. Recreation facilities include bathing, picnicking on the ocean beach (no tables or fireplaces); fishing area.

Park entrance on Island Beach. Garden State Parkway Exit 82 via Rte. 37.

120

OCEAN COUNTY SHORE RESORTS

Some resort communities restrict their beaches to residents only. Those for public use are listed below. State Marinas at Point Pleasant and Forked River; boat liveries, restaurants, amusement areas, hotel and motel accommodations available. Write: Ocean County Shore Resorts, Publicity Director, Washington St., Toms River, N.J. 08753.

Point Pleasant Beach
2-mile beach, swimming pool, fishing, boating, golf, horseback riding.

Lavalette
One and one-half mile beach, children's beaches, surf fishing, crabbing and boating in bay, tennis courts.

Seaside Heights
Patrolled beach, fishing, boardwalk, amusements, large children's amusement area.

Seaside Park
Patrolled beach, swimming pool, boating, fishing, crabbing, tennis.

All resorts accessible from Garden State Parkway, or Rtes. 9 and 70.

Ocean Gate
One mile beach on bay. Playground, boating, fishing.

Pine Beach
Small bay beach, boat rentals. Home of Admiral Farragut Academy.

Long Beach Island (Beach Haven, Long Beach Township, Ship Bottom, Surf City, Harvey Cedars, Barnegat Light)
18 miles of beach, ocean and bay swimming, fishing, boating, recreational facilities.

Barnegat Light Museum
Central Ave., Barnegat Light, N.J. 08006
Hours: daily, 2–5, July–Labor Day; weekends in June. Admission free.
Museum in former one-room school contains original lighthouse lens, plus local curios.

Commercial Fishing Docks

Barnegat Light, N.J. 08006

Hours: daily. Admission free.

Commercial fishing fleets, private, and charter boats operate from Myers Yacht Basin, 6th St. and the Bay, and the independent Dock Co., 18th St. and the Bay.

Foundation of the Arts and Sciences

Loveladies, N.J.

Hours: daily, 9 A.M.–10 P.M., July–Labor Day. Admission free; membership, $10.

Founded by Boris Blai, noted sculptor and former Dean of Tyler School of Fine Art. Visitors may view exhibits of painting, sculpture, and ceramic arts.

Wildlife Sanctuary

Holgate, N.J.

Hours: daily. Admission free.

Operated by the U.S. Department of the Interior. An unspoiled stretch of natural beach extends about 1½ miles from the end of the paved highway to the southern tip of the island.

BARNEGAT LIGHTHOUSE STATE PARK

c/o Island Beach State Park, Seaside Park, N.J. 08752 Tel.: (609) 494-2161

Hours: Daily, May 30–Labor Day; Sat., Sun., May 1–30 and Labor Day–Oct. 31. Fees: parking; entrance.

Park includes bathing, fishing and picnic facilities (no fires permitted). Site of country's second oldest lighthouse, which was designed by George Gordon Meade, the lighthouse construction began, under his supervision, in 1857. Six years later, as the general commanding the Army of the Potomac, General Meade earned his place in history with the victory of Gettysburg. For an additional 10¢ visitors may climb the circular staircase to top of the tower for a view of Barnegat Inlet and surrounding area. The lighthouse is no longer operative.

SCHOONER "LUCY EVELYN"

Beach Haven, N.J.

Hours: June 10–Sept. 10, daily, 10–10; rest of year, 10–5:30. Free admission to shop; admission fee to deck.

Once a cargo schooner, beached vessel houses gift and accessory shop. Children may explore deck of sailing ship. Surrounded by complex of gift, apparel, candle, flower shops. Eating facilities.

SIGHTSEEING CRUISES

Beach Haven, N.J. Tel.: (609) 492-2394

Hours: daily (see text), late June–Labor Day. Fee: varies with length.

Sightseeing cruises through Inland Waterway on "Inlet Starn." All-day trip with 6-hour stopover in Atlantic City: leaves 8:45, returns 7:15. Morning cruise: 8:45–1:30 with half-hour stopover. Moonlight cruise: 8:30–10 with no stopover.

From Beachhaven City Dock to Capt. Starn's Inlet Pier, Atlantic City.

SECTION 5

Camden
Gloucester
Atlantic

Camden County was the home of Walt Whitman, the "good gray poet," and of Betsy Ross who is said to have sewn the first American flag. Dolly Madison, wife of the fourth President of the United States, was a frequent visitor at the Indian King Tavern in Haddonfield when it was owned by her uncle. In 1623 the Dutch established the first European settlement in New Jersey at Fort Nassau, now Gloucester City. The first settler in what is now the city of Camden was probably William Cooper; the site of his cabin, built in 1681, may still be seen at Pyne Point. Also in 1681, Quaker families scattered throughout the area established a Meeting that is still in existence; it was the third Meeting to be established in New Jersey. More than a hundred years later, William Cooper's descendant Jacob laid out the present city of Camden, naming it in honor of Charles Pratt, Earl of Camden, an English judge who had befriended the Colonies.

Gloucester County, which originally included all of Camden and Atlantic, was created in 1686. The area was settled, after the original Dutch arrivals, by Swedes and English. The most notable action in Gloucester during the Revolution was that at Fort Mercer in 1777, where five hundred hungry, ragged Rhode Island Volunteers held off two thousand Hessians. Meanwhile, American guns, mounted on barges, sank the British ships *August* and *Merlin*, but not quickly enough to prevent them from firing into a farm house near the fort. As the battle raged, Mrs. Anna Cooper Whitall sat calmly spinning inside her house. Suddenly a cannonball blasted into the room, past the imperturbable Quaker lady. Quietly she collected her wheel and yarn and retired to the cellar, where she continued to spin. Later she scolded Hessian prisoners, as she bound their wounds, for coming to America to kill innocent colonists.

Most of Gloucester was ocean bed at one time, and its extensive marl beds (hence the name Marlboro) are valuable as fertilizer, water softening, and in glass manufacture. The county ranks next to California in the growing of asparagus and has some of New Jersey's finest orchards.

The area that is now Atlantic County was settled in 1679, near Egg Harbor City, and the county was created in 1837. In case you've ever wondered why Little Egg Harbor is bigger than Big Egg Harbor, it is because the hungry explorers found big eggs in the small harbor and little eggs in the big one.

Commander Richard Somers of the U.S. Navy, who commanded the explosive-loaded *Intrepid* when it was sent to destroy the enemy fleet at Tripoli in 1804, was a member of the family for whom Somers Point was named. His birthplace, Somers Mansion, has been restored and may now be visited.

Egg Harbor City is the birthplace of the famous "Jersey Devil," a legendary monster with a collie's head, a horse face, and the body of a kangaroo. This devil is mild, playful, woman-shy, and a loner. It has not been seen by many people, but this does not detract from the firm belief that many South Jerseyites have in him. In fact, when he was reported to have moved to Chester County, Pennsylvania, the uproar was thunderous as natives demanded his return.

Atlantic City, with its beautiful beaches and extensive boardwalk, is a world-renowned resort and convention site. The surrounding area offers fine fishing and boating, while inland the rich soil produces cranberries, peaches, lettuce, asparagus and many other truck and orchard crops.

View of Camden from Philadelphia's Walnut St. wharf, 1845

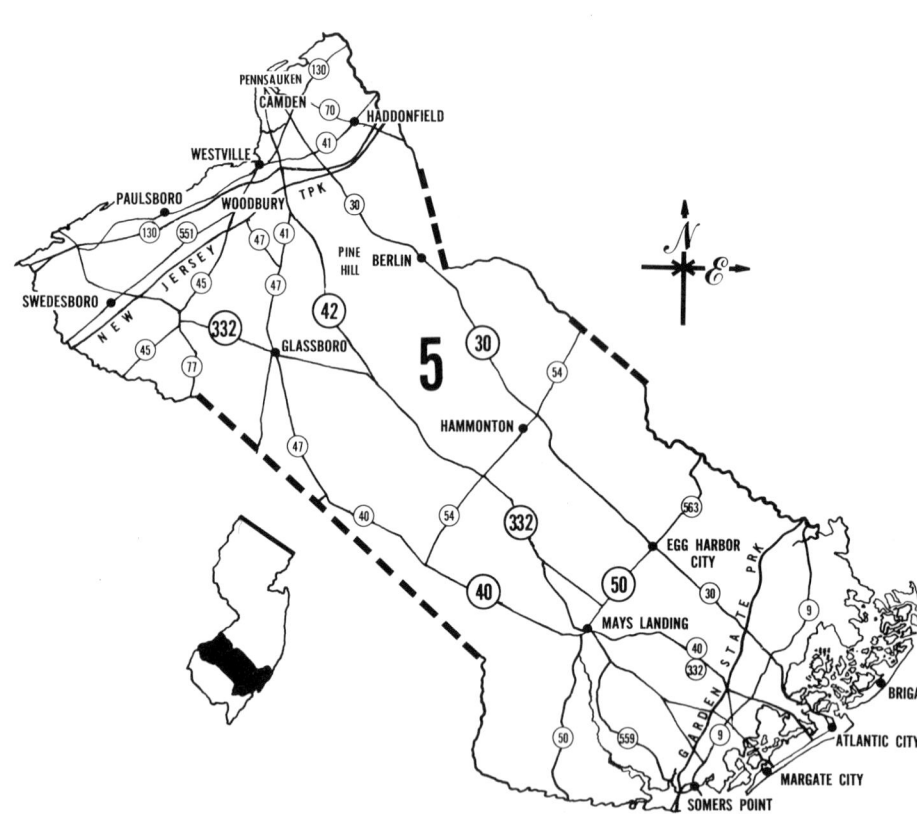

HUNTER-LAWRENCE HOUSE

58 N. Broad St., Woodbury, N.J.   Tel.: (609) 845-4771

Hours: Wed., 1–4; Fri., 7–9:30; by appointment. Admission free.

This old home is the headquarters for the museum and library of the Gloucester County Historical Society. The 17-room museum houses many fine collections of Indian relics, furniture, toys, farm tools, glass, war artifacts, etc. The 6,000-volume library is known for its fine collection of genealogical and historical material on the South Jersey area.

In the center of Woodbury, opposite Central School.

MORAVIAN CHURCH

Kings Highway, Swedesboro, N.J.   Tel.: (609) 467-0290

Hours: by reservation only. Admission free.

Brick structure, built 1786 by Moravian sect, to replace earlier log church. Now maintained as historical shrine by Gloucester County Historical Society. Luncheon facilities in Swedesboro.

From N.J. Turnpike, southbound, right at Interchange #2; left on Rte. 551 to Swedesboro. Church property on Sharptown Rd., two miles south of Swedesboro.

PENNSAUKEN TOUR

This southern New Jersey town has several noteworthy old houses. Those listed below are either private residences or are in process of restoration and repair. For a tour of the interiors, make a reservation with the Pennsauken Historical Society, 6711 Grant Ave., Pennsauken, N.J. 08109.

Burrough-Dover House

9201 Burrough-Dover Lane

Restored by the Pennsauken Historical Society, this house was built in two parts (about 1710 and 1793). It is an early American farm house with appropriate furnishings.

Off Haddonfield Rd. near the Mart.

Burrough-Purvis House (private residence)

8359 Maple Ave.

For visit, see above.

Built by Burrough family in 1770 and once served as an inn.

West of the south branch of Pennsauken Creek.

Pennsville School
Rte. 130, Westfield Ave. at Haddonfield Rd.

Excellent example of 19th-century one-room schoolhouse.

Burrough-Laurence House (private residence)
Colonial and Irving Aves.

For visit, see above.

Built of Jersey brown sandstone about 1728. Has hip-roof section; nearby smokehouse.

Off Haddonfield Road.

TRINITY EPISCOPAL CHURCH
Kings Highway and Church St., Swedesboro, N.J. Tel.: 467-0290 (Rectory)

Hours: daylight. Admission free.

Historic church, formerly Swedish Evangelical Lutheran Church, built 1784 by Swedish colonists. Contains historical documents and relics.

Turnpike, southbound; right at Interchange 2; left on Rte. 551.

FRIENDS' MEETING HOUSE
North Broad St., Woodbury, N.J. Tel.: (609) 845-5080

Hours: by reservation only. Admission free.

Still active Quaker meeting house. Many first settlers and patriots interred in burial grounds.

In Woodbury center.

NATIONAL PARK AND RED BANK BATTLEFIELD
Rte. 44, Westville, N.J.

Hours: daily. Admission free.

20-acre park containing remains of Fort Mercer. Here the British fleet was prevented from sailing up the Delaware during the Revolution. Picnic facilities.

Ann Whitall House
100 Hessian Ave., National Park, N.J. Tel.: (609) 845-4318

Hours: Sat., Sun., 2–4. Fee: 25¢. Tour: school groups, by reservation; free.

Built in 1748, this house still bears the scars from the Battle of Red Bank. It was used as a hospital for wounded Hessians and Americans. Period furnishings and battle artifacts.

Boys inspecting royal coat of arms on cannon

Red Bank Battlefield

100 Hessian Ave., National Park, N.J. Tel.: (609) 845-4318
Hours: daily, 9–6. Admission free.
This 20-acre battlefield was placed under the care of the Gloucester County Freeholders by Act of Congress in 1905. Trenches, cannons, monuments on the grounds are of special interest. Parking; restrooms; large picnic area.

West on Hessian Ave. from No. Broad St., Woodbury, N.J.

CAMDEN HISTORICAL SOCIETY

Park Blvd. and Euclid Ave., Camden, N.J. Tel.: (609) 964-3333
Hours: Museum, Mon.–Fri., 9–12, 1–4:30. Library, closed Sat. and Mon.; other days, 12:30–4:30. Groups by reservation. Admission free.

Pomona Hall–Joseph Cooper Jr. House (museum)

Headquarters of the Society; built in 1726 and added to in 1788. Furnished with antiques of the period. On second floor are reproductions of trade shops of the era: blacksmith, cobbler, wheelwright, etc., with antique tools.

Library and Auditorium

Both structures built to conform architecturally with the Museum. Library houses collections of Revolutionary, 1812, Civil War uniforms; saddles; muskets; etc. Contains historical documents; genealogical material of South Jersey; U.S. history.

From N.J. Turnpike, Exit 4; west on Rte. 38 to Park Blvd.; left to Euclid.

WALT WHITMAN HOUSE

330 Mickle St., Camden, N.J.   Tel.: (609) 964-5383

Hours: Tues.–Sat. and holidays, 10–12, 1–5; Sun., 2–5. Fee: adults, 25¢; children under 12, free.

Poet's house; 3 rooms furnished with his possessions. Collections of manuscripts, photographs and library of his works.

From N.J. Turnpike, Exit 4; turn right on Rte. 38 to 2nd St.; then right on Mickle St.

Sleigh riding past Indian King Tavern

INDIAN KING TAVERN

233 King's Highway East, Haddonfield, N.J. Tel.: (609) 429-6792

Hours: Tues.–Sat., and holidays, 10–12, 1–5; Sun., 2–5. Fee: adults, 25¢; children under 12, free. Tour: reservations for groups required.

State-owned inn, built 1750; the State Legislature held frequent meetings in this tavern. Here the Council for Safety for New Jersey was organized in 1777 and the Great Seal of New Jersey was received and adopted. Now a National Historic Site.

From N.J. Turnpike, Exit 4; Rte. 73 west; Rte. 41 south to Ellisburg; east on Rte. 70.

HADDON FIRE CO. #1 MUSEUM

King's Highway and Haddon Ave., Haddonfield, N.J. 08033 Tel.: (609) 429-2400.

Hours: daily; visitors welcome any hour. Admission free.

Company #1 is second oldest volunteer fire company in continuous operation, in the U.S. (oldest is in Mt. Holly); started Mar. 8, 1764. Company maintains small museum containing old helmets, implements. Has two early fire engines: one hand-drawn, one horse-drawn. Visitors also given a tour of the company's modern fire fighting equipment.

GREENFIELD HALL

343 King's Highway East, Haddonfield, N.J. 08033 Tel.: (609) 429-7375

Hours: Tues. and Thurs., 2–4:30 and by appointment. Closed July–Aug. Admission free.

Hall is the old Gill House, built partly in 1747 and completed in 1841. Personal items of Elizabeth Haddon, town's first settler (1713). Boxwood garden; period furniture; costumes; research library. Home of Historical Society of Haddonfield.

The Hip Roof House

In process of restoration by Society. Elizabeth Haddon owned it for 12 years; erected circa 1742.

Rte. 70 to King's Highway; one block from Indian King Tavern.

L. N. RENAULT & SONS, INC. (winery)

P.O. Box 364, Egg Harbor City, N.J. 08215. Tel.: (609) 965-2111

Hours: Mon.–Sat., 9–6; open year round. Admission free. Conducted tours.

Bottling, storage plants for wines, champagne. Especially fine to visit in first 3 weeks of Sept. when grapes are crushed. Hospitality center, wine tasting. Glass museum; wine cellars; gift shop. For adults and children 10 years and up. Call or write for group reservations.

ELEPHANT HOUSE
Atlantic Ave. at Decatur, Margate City, N.J.

Hours: under restoration. For information, write "Elephant, Margate, N.J. 08402."

Elephant-shaped, six story building, built 1881. Used as observatory.

On Atlantic Ave., south of Atlantic City.

PINE HILL SKI MOUNTAIN AREA
DeCou Road and Branch Ave., Pine Hill, N.J. 08021   Tel.: (609) 783-8484

Hours: daily, 10–5, 6–11; weekends, holidays, 9 A.M.*–11* P.M. *Fees: vary.*

Snow-making equipment. Rentals; ski school; clinic for high school, college and groups; no lodging. Restaurant; nursery.

South of Rte. 534, in Pine Hill.

FARMERS' AUCTION MARKET
Market St., Glassboro, N.J.

Hours: mornings, April–Nov. Admission free.

Farm produce and farm supplies auctioned off. Interesting to those over 10. Luncheon facilities in Glassboro.

From N.J. Turnpike, southbound; Interchange #3. Take Rte. 42, then Rte. 41 to Glassboro. Pass High School, turn on Market St.

ATLANTIC CITY
World famous seaside resort. Open all year. There are lifeguard supervised ocean swimming, beaches, bathhouses, indoor and outdoor swimming pools, fishing and sail boating. Rolling chairs for hire for Boardwalk sightseeing and bicycles for rent. Horseback riding on the beach from Oct. until May. Sightseeing by boat, bus, rolling chair, or seaplane. Noteworthy sights in boardwalk area include:

Absecon Hall—built in 1854 and now restored.

Convention Hall—tours available.

Garden Pier—civic center with free band concerts weekly.

Million Dollar Pier—amusements.

Steel Pier—amusements, marine ballroom, 2 movie theatres.
Open daily during summer.

Steeplechase Pier—charges for amusements.

ATLANTIC CITY MARINA
600 Huron Blvd., Atlantic City, N.J.
On Clam Creek, state-operated marina: 12-foot draft; 406 berths; accommodates 120-foot lengths.

ABSECON LIGHTHOUSE (State Restoration)
Pacific and Rhode Island Avenues, Atlantic City, N.J.
Hours: daily except Mon., 10–5 weekdays; Sun., 12–5. Open summer months. Fee for admission.
Historic lighthouse was commissioned in 1857 and in use until 1933. 167 feet high, its light was visible 19 miles at sea.

CAPTAIN STARN'S INLET PIER
Maine and Caspian Aves., Atlantic City, N.J.   Tel.: (609) 344-3905
Hours: daily from Mar. 1, some evenings; reservations suggested. Fee: prices vary; see text.
Sightseeing trips: Easter–Oct. 15, leaving on the half-hour. Some moonlight cruises. Costs range from $1.25 for children on sail trips, to $4.50 for adults on half-day fishing trips. Rods and reels for rent. Live fish aquarium; sea lion exhibit; curio shop; fish market. Free parking; eating facilities.
From Absecon Blvd., east to Melrose Ave.; to Maine Ave. on ocean; then north.

SOMERS MANSION
Somers Point, N.J. 08244   Tel.: (609) 921-2212
Hours: Tues.–Sat., 10–12, 2–5; Sun., 2–5. Fee: adults, 25¢; children under 12, free. Tours: reservations for groups required.
This 230-year-old mansion restored to original condition. Birthplace of Richard Somers, USN, killed in Tripoli, 1804. Headquarters of the Atlantic County Historical Society; includes displays relating to historical shore area. Parking at the mansion; restaurants nearby.
Rte. 52; north of Ocean City.

HISTORIC SMITHVILLE INN

Rte. 9, Smithville, N.J. 08201   Tel.: (609) 641-7777

Hours: Village, 10:30–10:30; Inns 11:30–10. Tours: groups by reservation only.

The original Inn, built in 1787, is the center of an old South Jersey restoration. Village has numerous shops, many in carefully restored houses: General stores, tobacconist, sweet shop, clam shack, etc. Animal farm for children. Free winter sleigh rides, stagecoach rides, summer hay rides. Inns serve luncheon buffet and dinner. "Posset Shop" serves breakfast, lunch and snacks.

Garden State Parkway Exit 48 to Rte. 9; 6 miles north of Absecon.

Part of Village at Smithville Inn

SECTION 6

Salem
Cumberland
Cape May

Salem is the Hebrew word for peace, and when John Fenwick brought his family and a group of fellow Quakers to settle in West Jersey in 1675, he called the land New Salem. It brought little peace to Fenwick, who became involved in numerous financial problems, but as William Penn's first settlement of Friends on the eastern side of the Delaware, it grew and prospered. It was the land of tranquility to Catholic, Lutheran, and other Protestant farmers who sought religious freedom among the original Quaker settlers. The soil was exceedingly rich and the farmers were happy as they turned the county into a garden spot and raised enormous cattle during the following years.

The winter of 1778 saw the American forces literally starving at Valley Forge. In February, General "Mad Anthony" Wayne led a foraging party to Salem in search of its famous cattle, and they collected over three hundred head, returning to Valley Forge through Haddonfield and Trenton, making a defiant, mocking show toward the British. This enraged the enemy, who sent Colonel Charles Mahwood and Major John Graves Simcoe to "chastise the rascals." The Americans retreated to Alloway's Creek, where at Quinton's Bridge on March 18, they repulsed the British. At dawn three days later, Major Simcoe led a group of Hessians and Tories against the house of Judge William Hancock, at Hancock's Bridge. Attacking without warning, they massacred thirty Americans sleeping there, many of whom were personal acquaintances of the murdering Tories.

After the Revolution, the overworked soil of Salem could not support all of the people, and many Salemites joined the great migration westward. Among them were Zadok Street and his son, who were so homesick for their county that on their way they founded Salems in Ohio, Indiana, and Iowa, and finally ended the migration with Salem, Oregon.

In the 1820's, the discovery of marl as a fertilizer gradually gave the farms a new lease on life, slowing down the migration. Salem's farmers again raised the huge pigs and cattle. The most famous of Salem's enormous specimens was Job Taylor's ox, which, in 1823, yielded 2,652 pounds of beef, tallow, and hide.

The coming of the railroad in 1865 brought a resurgence of the colonial glass industry, which today plays a large part in the economy of Salem. The county has a strong link with the past in the more than 150 pre-Revolutionary houses scattered throughout the county, preserved with love and respect.

Cumberland County, "tidewater country" to those who love it, resembles Delaware and Maryland more than the rest of New Jersey. The county seat, until 1748 when Cumberland was carved out of Salem, was Greenwich, where settlers laid out the town along "Ye Greate Streete" of John Fenwick's dreams, one hundred feet wide and two miles long. Here the economy of the county centered during the late 1700's, so it was a natural place for the English merchant captain J. Allen to deposit the cargo of tea which he hoped to smuggle into New York and Philadelphia. Word got around to the townspeople who, in this year of 1774, had sworn with most of New Jersey never to drink tea while unjust taxes were imposed by Britain. A group of young men disguised themselves as Indians and dragged the chests of

Cape May Point Lighthouse

137

tea from the cellar of the Tory Van Bowen, where it was hidden, into the village square for a bonfire.

An interesting sidelight to New Jersey's own tea party was that one of its young leaders, Richard Howell, after fighting in the Revolution, went on to become governor of the state. His daughter Verona married Jefferson Davis, president of the Confederacy.

During the Revolution, the section which later became Cumberland was a prime food supplier—in fact, General Washington declared that his army could not have survived Valley Forge without the produce of its farms. Today Cumberland is still great farming country. Vineland, known as "the egg basket of the nation," supplies the metropolitan markets to the north and west. The glass industry, dating from Colonial times, is large and important, and Cumberland's extensive oyster farms make oyster-lovers happy all along the seaboard.

Cape May County is said to have more Mayflower descendants than Plymouth County, Massachusetts. This is because of the large influx around 1785 of New England whalers, many of whom were descendants of the Pilgrims. But this is not how the county got its name, for it was created in 1692. The cape at the southern end of the state was named by that far-wandering Dutch captain, Cornelius Jacobsen Mey, who decided that its climate was like that of his native land (a great compliment).

Whaling furnished a more and more precarious livelihood and by 1700 Cape May had become a farming and fishing community. Captain Kidd is one of the many pirates believed to have buried treasure somewhere along the shore, and to this day adults and children search for it. What they usually find are "Cape May diamonds," bits of pure quartz rounded by the action of the water—samples of a vast deposit of glass sand which underlies the whole area.

It was in 1801 that the first advertisement extolling the climate and sea bathing of Cape May was placed in a Philadelphia newspaper, and thus began its great annual business. Cape May is still a farming and fishing community, but first and foremost, it is the "watering place" of New Jersey.

Giant holly tree on the Garden State Parkway near Seaville in Cape May County

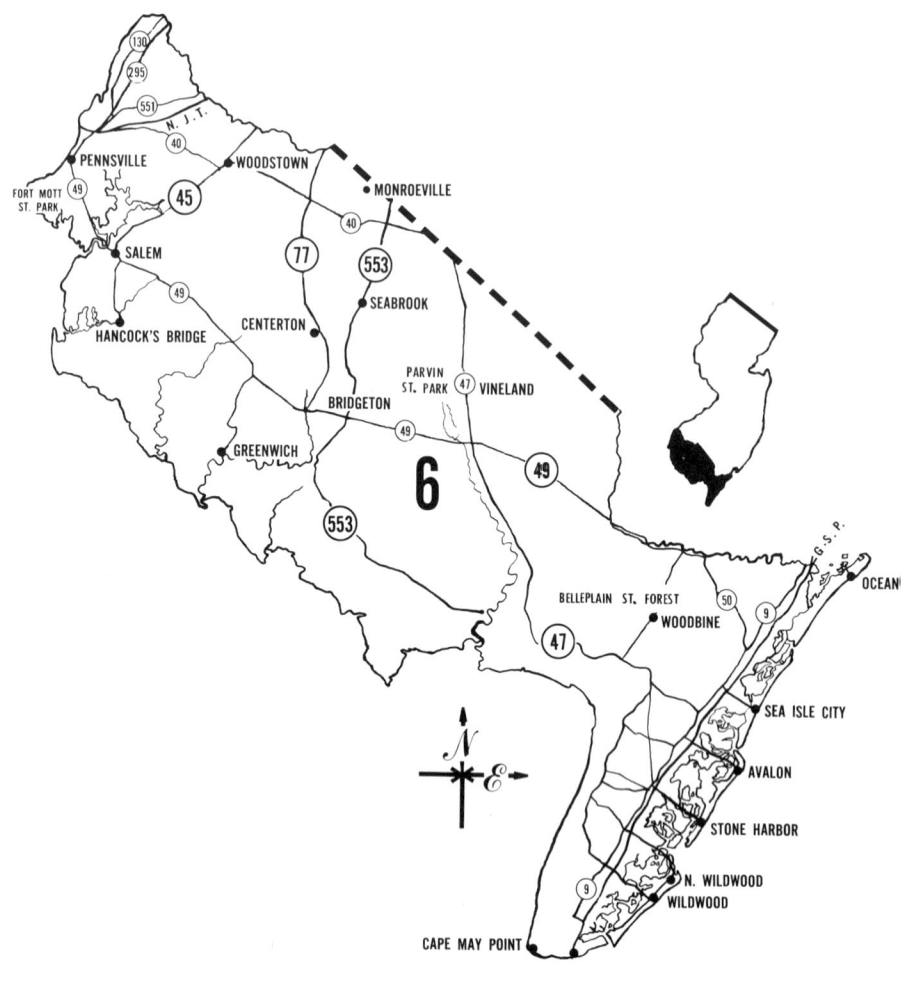

6

PENNSVILLE
FORT MOTT ST. PARK
N. J. T.
WOODSTOWN
MONROEVILLE
SALEM
SEABROOK
HANCOCK'S BRIDGE
CENTERTON
PARVIN ST. PARK
VINELAND
BRIDGETON
GREENWICH
BELLEPLAIN ST. FOREST
WOODBINE
OCEAN
SEA ISLE CITY
AVALON
STONE HARBOR
N. WILDWOOD
WILDWOOD
CAPE MAY POINT

N E

FORT MOTT STATE PARK
R.D. 3, Salem, N.J. 08079   Tel.: (609) 935-3218
Hours: daily. Fees: picnic table, fireplace.

At Finn's Point, the park affords an excellent view of the lower Delaware River. One of forts built to guard the river below Philadelphia. Finn's Point National Cemetery nearby. Facilities include fishing and picnicking.

CUMBERLAND HISTORICAL SOCIETY
P.O. Box 16, Greenwich, N.J. 08323
Tours: see text.

Gibbon House
Main Street, Greenwich.
Hours: Sat., Sun., 2–5, first Sunday in April–last Sunday in Oct. Fee: nonmembers, adults and children over 12, 25¢.

Built in 1730, the house contains a collection of memorabilia, artifacts, clothing, china, silverware from colonial days to Civil War. Research book collection of Dr. Everett Tomlinson on New Jersey history. For time reservation, call (609) 451-8454 or 451-5374.

Red Barn Museum
Behind Gibbon House

Collection of Indian and settler artifacts. Utensils, clothing, implements, from colonial to Civil War days. Look for surprise in old coffin.

Lecture and Exhibit Hall
Main St.

Lecture on Greenwich, history, use of artifacts in the Cumberland Historical Society's collection. Different exhibits of privately owned antique collections shown every Sunday, April–October. Tours start here. Call (609) 451-8454 for reservation.

Cohansey Baptist Graveyard
Off Sheppards Mill Road
First settler child born in area (1683) buried here.

Greenwich Walking Tour

This lovely old town, site of the New Jersey Tea Burning Party, has many beautiful old houses lovingly preserved and carefully researched by the Cumberland Historical Society. Interiors may be viewed only once every two years; for information, call (609) 451-8454. For walking tour guide information, call (609) 455-2191.

Main Street
(Start walk at water's edge)

Mark Reeve House
Earliest home in Greenwich. Oldest section built in 1686.

Friends' Meeting House
Open Sundays, 2–5, April–Oct.

Tea Burning Monument
Set in little park, corner of Main and Market Lane.

Harding House
Believed to have been built before 1734.

Dr. Holme's House
Behind a gasoline pump but worth seeing.

Pirate House
Built in 1734 and said to have resident ghost.

Richard Wood Mansion
House has been in the Wood family since its erection in 1795.

Old Schoolhouse
Occupied by Society of New Jersey Artists. Oldest schoolhouse in area (1810).

Old Store Tavern
Earliest accommodation in area for man "and his beaste" (1728).

Sheppards Mill Road

Dr. T. Stathem House
Lovely old brick and iron grillwork.

Drs. Ward and Fithian House
Built in 1760 of wood and beautifully preserved.

Richard Wood Mansion

YE OLDE CENTERTON INN

Centerton, N.J.   Tel.: (609) 358-3201

Hours: daily, 12–2, 5:30–9.

Built 1706, still in operation as restaurant. A Colonial stage-coach stop between Port Greenwich and Philadelphia. Early American paintings, furniture and documents. Country store, coach house.

On Rte. 533, north of Bridgeton.

DE COUS CERTIFIED FARM MARKET AND HILLTOP ORCHARDS, INC.

Shiloh, N.J. 08353   Tel.: (609) 451-7908 or 451-3729

Hours: June thru Dec., daily, 9 A.M.–dark. Fees: vary according to size; no charge for school groups. Tour: by reservation only; varies from 1–2 hours; no limit to numbers; number of adults required to accompany youngsters varies with size of group.

One of few remaining old-fashioned markets in the state. Tour includes packing and storage houses, outlying barns, pick-up truck ride to watch fruit being picked. Explanation of controlled atmosphere storage, participation in washing, sorting, packing.

On Rte. 49, between Bridgeton and Salem.

COWTOWN RODEO
Sharpstown, N.J. Tel.: (609) 769-3200 or 769-1118
Hours: telephone for information.
Rodeo contests, sanctioned by the National Rodeo Association.
About 2 miles west of Woodstown on U.S. 40.

SALEM COUNTY HISTORICAL SOCIETY
79, 81 and 83 Market St., Salem, N.J. 08079   Tel.: (609) 935-5004. If no answer, (609) 935-2377 (Mr. J. Trucksess, Librarian).
Hours: Tues.–Fri., 1–3 P.M. *Groups by reservation. Fee: donation, 75¢. Tour: guides available.*
Restored houses and a stone barn. Indian relics; rare glass, china; furniture; farm implements.

1736 John Jones Law Office
Earliest brick law office in the original 13 colonies.

Headquarters of the Salem County Historical Society

HANCOCK HOUSE

Hancock's Bridge, N.J. 08038   Tel.: (609) 935-4373

Hours: Tues.–Sat., 10–12, 1–5; Sun., 2–5. Fee: adults, 25¢; children under 12, free. Tour: reservations required.

House, built 1734, was scene of Patriot massacre by British and Tory troops during Revolution. Excellent period furnishings.

From Salem, 5 miles south on East Broadway. Follow signs.

BRIDGETON LIBERTY BELL

Cumberland County Court House, Broad St., Bridgeton, N.J.

Bell was cast in 1763 in Bridgewater, Mass., and was purchased by subscription by the Bridgeton residents. The liberty bell rang out the news of the signing of the Declaration of Independence from the cupola of the old Court House, atop Broad Street Hill.

OLD BROAD STREET CHURCH

Broad Street, Bridgeton, N.J.

Hours: June, July, Aug., Sundays only, 2–5.

Eighteenth-century brick church with Palladian window. Original furnishings throughout with wineglass pulpit, "All Seeing Eye of God," whale oil lamps, etc.

Old Broad Street Church

BRIDGETON CITY PARK
Bridgeton, N.J.

Hours: daily. Admission free.

Park area with three lakes; paths and driving roads. Canoes for hire. Picnic facilities.

Cohansey Zoo

Hours: year round. Fee: donation.

Interesting small zoo. Can be toured in about ½ hour.

LAKE GARRISON
Buck Rd., Elk Township, Monroeville, N.J. Tel.: (609) 881-2872

Hours: summers, daily, 9 A.M.–11 P.M. Fees: entrance and rentals; group rates.

Fresh water lake with swimming and boating. Rentals of canoes, rowboats, paddleboats. Picnic grounds; refreshment pavillion.

Rte. 553 from Glassboro center; south on North Main St. to Buck Rd.; 4 miles on Buck Rd.

Nail House Museum

THE NAIL HOUSE MUSEUM

West Commerce Street entrance to Bridgeton City Park, Bridgeton, N.J.

Hours: Sundays only, 2–5.

Small museum of the Bridgeton Antiquarian League, in original office of local nail industry. Contains exhibits of South Jersey glass; iron banks and toys; nail cutting machine; one of the oldest public clocks in New Jersey.

KIMBLE GLASS CO.

Crystal Ave., Vineland, N.J. 08360   Tel.: (609) 692-3600

Hours: by reservation. Phone or write: Personnel Dept. Admission free. Tour: for age 14 and up; one hour.

Tour shows glass blowers at work. Eating facilities nearby.

PARVIN STATE PARK

R.D. 1, Elmer, N.J. 08318   Tel.: (609) 692-7039

Hours: Daily, May 30–Labor Day; May 1–30 and Labor Day–Oct. 31, Sat., Sun. Fees: entrance; parking; boat rentals; bathing.

This state park contains a rich variety of flora and bird life. Facilities include bathing; boating; canoeing; hiking; picnicking; camping; fishing. Cabins available on Thundergust Pond and campsites on Parvin Lake. Boat and canoe rentals.

6 mi. west of Vineland, just east of the intersection of Rtes. 540 and 553.

BELLEPLAIN STATE FOREST AND LAKE NUMMY
Woodbine, N.J. Tel.: (609) 861-2404

Hours: Daily, May 30–Labor Day; Sat., Sun., May 1–30 and Labor Day–Oct. 31. Fees for entrance, parking, motorless boats.

Lake Nummy is the principal developed recreation area. Facilities include bathing, picnicking, camping, hunting and fishing.

Garden State Parkway Exit 17 via Rte. 550 or Exit 13 via Rtes. 9 and 550.

CAPE MAY BEACH RESORTS
Avalon, Cape May City, Ocean City, Sea Isle City, Stone Harbor, The Wildwoods

For information, write for free booklet, "Cape May County Resort Guide," Cape May County Leader Co., Inc., Wildwood, N.J.

The above "N.J. Cape" resorts offer public swimming from protected beaches; fishing from beach, pier, or party boat; boardwalk recreation and children's playgrounds. Weekly and annual sailing regattas. Golf at Ocean City Golf Club at Somers Point and Wildwood Golf and Country Club.

All may be reached from Garden State Parkway.

OCEAN CITY HISTORICAL MUSEUM
409 Wesley Ave., Ocean City, N.J. 08226

Hours: Winter, Tues.–Sat., 1–4; summer, Mon.–Sat., 10–4. Admission free. Tours: groups by reservation.

Within the museum proper is a completely furnished Ocean City home of the 19th century. Other parts of the museum house pictures, documents, maps, etc., of the period 1890–1910. Indian artifacts; shells; fossils; stone collection; mounted bird collection; decoys. Sindia Room houses ship models, prints, photos, sailing papers and the figurehead of the 4-masted bark *Sindia,* sunk during a gale in 1901.

CAPE MAY COUNTRY STORE
Jefferson and Page Sts., Cape May, N.J.

Hours: daily, from 10.

Re-creation of Colonial country store. Watch candles being made; butter churned, etc. Many unusual displays.

Making candles in Cape May Country Store

CONVENTION HALL

Beach Ave., Cape May, N.J.

Visitors are advised to inquire at information desk for town activities. Convention Hall features concerts, dancing, contests, and other entertainment.

COAST GUARD RECRUIT TRAINING CENTER

Cape May, N.J. 08210   Tel.: (609) 884-8451

Hours: Fri., 1:30–2:30—graduation exercises; Armed Forces Week.

Graduation exercises, open to public, every Friday. For information on tour of facilities, write Commanding Officer; no tours without advance appointment.

CAPE MAY COUNTY HISTORICAL MUSEUM

Cape May Court House, N.J. 08210   Tel.: (609) 465-7111

Hours: daily, 9–12, 12:30–4; closed holidays. Fee: donation.

Story of early settlers told through exhibits. Informed attendant to answer questions. Exhibits include: County Shop Lane; "Arts, Domestic and Imported for the American Home"; Colonial kitchen; whaling; early county artifacts; Silas Matthew's Period Room: stenciled room, circa 1790, with period furniture.

CAPE MAY COUNTY PARK

U.S. Route 9.

Hours: June–Aug., 9–9; Sept.–May, 9–dusk.

Picnic facilities, grills. Nature trail, archery, children's playgrounds, shuffleboard, horseshoes, quoits, volleyball, badminton, croquet, tetherball, tennis, hopscotch, bocce.

North on Rte. 9; approx. 2 miles from Cape May Court House.

CAPE MAY POINT

Cape May, N.J.

Hours: daily, May–Sept.

Beach area at southern tip of state. Gift shop and luncheon facilities. Interesting features include:

Bird Sanctuary

Haven for smaller migratory birds, especially in Aug. when northbound flights begin. Picturesque setting, with Spanish oaks, and other southern species not found elsewhere in N.J.

Northwest Magnesite Co.

Producer of magnesite, used in refractory furnace brick, from sea water and dolomite.

"Atlantis"

Wreck of concrete ship.

Cape May "Diamonds"

Amateur geologists can find these clear silicate pebbles on the beach. When cut and polished they resemble diamonds.

From Garden State Parkway, Exit 0; drive through Cape May City; follow signs to Sunset Beach and Cape May Point.

STONE HARBOR BIRD SANCTUARY

Stone Harbor, N.J.

Sanctuary maintained by Borough of Stone Harbor. Over 5,000 birds, mostly egrets, herons, related species.

Note: Nature lectures with slides or colored movies, 2nd and 4th Mondays during July and Aug. For information write: Witmer Stone Club, Stone Harbor, N.J. 08247.

SECTION 7

Philadelphia

New Jersey residents are urged to include nearby Philadelphia in their list of day trip "musts." It is accessible from anywhere in the state by excellent roads, particularly the N.J. Turnpike.

The city ranks among the foremost of American cities in size, commercial and cultural development, historical background, and present-day importance.

Founded in 1682 by William Penn, it grew to prominence prior to the American Revolution and served as the nation's capital from 1790–1800. Today, Philadelphia is a city of contrasts, blending its illustrious past with its ultramodern city-of-tomorrow look. Noted for its shipping, manufacturing, and the center of many scientific, cultural and artistic institutions and societies, Philadelphia has revitalized its downtown area as it plans for the celebration, in 1976, of the nation's 200th birthday.

Whether you plan a visit for a day, or longer, Philadelphia offers something for everyone, for every taste, for every age, for every pocketbook.

The place to begin your visit, for complete information, maps, things to do and see:

PHILADELPHIA CONVENTION AND TOURIST BUREAU
Tourist Center
16th and John F. Kennedy Blvd.
Philadelphia, Pa. 19102
Tel.: (215) 561-1200 or 665-1976

FAIRMOUNT PARK TOUR

Park reached via the Benjamin Franklin Parkway, from the heart of Philadelphia. Telephone (215) PO 5-0500, Philadelphia Museum of Art, Park Houses Office, to make arrangements to see Mount Pleasant, Cedar Grove, Lemon Hill and other historic houses in the Park. The following institutions are located near, or within its borders.

Franklin Institute

Twentieth and Parkway. Tel.: (215) LO 4-3838

Hours: weekdays, 10–5; Sun., 12–5. Fees: adults, $1.25; children, 95¢.

Museum of Science and Technology. Scientific apparatus arranged as do-it-yourself exhibits; locomotives; airplanes.

Fels Planetarium

Hours: weekdays, 3; Sat., 11, 1, 2, 3. Sun., 2, 3, 4; Wed., Fri., evenings at 8. Fee: included in Institute fee.

Academy of Natural Sciences

Nineteenth and Parkway. Tel.: (215) LO 4-3921

Hours: weekdays, 10–5; Sun., 1–5. Fees: adults, 75¢; children under 12, 35¢; group rates.

Oldest scientific institution of its kind in the U.S. Animal life groups; birds indigenous to Philadelphia area; minerals; Fluorescence exhibit; Hall of Earth History. Free nature films for children, Saturday mornings. Live animal shows: Mon.–Fri., 10:15, 12:45; Sat., Sun., 2 and 3.

Philadelphia Museum of Art

26th St. and Parkway

Hours: daily, 9–5; closed major legal holidays. Fee: adults, 50¢; children, 25¢; free: Mondays, all day; Sundays, 9–1. Foreign language tours: by appointment.

Paintings; sculpture; American fashions; period rooms; oriental art.

Rodin Museum

22nd St. and Parkway. Tel.: (215) PO 5-0500

Hours: daily, 9–5. Fee: Tues.–Sun., 25¢; children under 12, free; no charge on Mondays.

Largest collection of Rodin sculpture outside France. Also, artist's watercolors, drawings.

Robin Hood Dell Concerts

Fairmount Park (near Ridge and Huntington Sts.)

Hours: Mon., Tues., Thurs., 8:30 P.M. mid-June through July. Children's concerts, 3 Wednesdays, 11 A.M. Admission free. Reservations: three weeks notice required; write, enclosing stamped, self-addressed envelope, Dept. of Recreation, P.O. Box 1930, Philadelphia, Pa. 19105.

Philadelphia Orchestra; guest conductors; soloists. Natural outdoor amphitheatre.

Note: children under 12 not admitted to evening concerts; young people, 12–16, with adults only.

INDEPENDENCE HALL

Chestnut Street. Tel.: (215) 597-7018

Hours: daily, 8:45–5. Admission free.

State House of the Colony and Commonwealth of Pennsylvania until 1799. In Assembly Room, Declaration of Independence was adopted; here Articles of Constitution were drafted in 1787. West Chamber is court room of Pennsylvania's Supreme Court. Liberty Bell in stair tower.

Between Fifth and Sixth Sts. on Chestnut.

AMERICAN WAX MUSEUM

Bourse Building, Independence Mall. Tel.: (215) MA 7-6677

Hours: weekdays, 9:30–5; Sat., Sun., 9:30–5:30. Fee: adults, $1.50; children under 14, 75¢; servicemen, 75¢.

100 life-sized figures in dramatic tableaux depicting great moments in American history with action, sound, light and color.

5th Street between Chestnut and Market Sts.

PHILADELPHIA MARITIME MUSEUM

427 Chestnut St.

Hours: weekdays, 10–4 (June 15–Sept. 14, 10–5); Sun., 12–5. Fee: adults, 50¢; children 5–12, 25¢; group rates.

U.S. maritime history, particularly that of port of Philadelphia. Ship models; paintings; prints; shipmaker's tools; navigator's instruments; charts; weapons.

Note: The following are not open to public (see text for details) but are worth viewing from outside.

Rear view of Independence Hall

Second Bank of the United States (Old Customs House)
420 Chestnut St.

Closed for restoration: check Visitor's Center, Independence National Historical Park, 116 South Third St. for opening.

Designed by William Strickland in Greek Revival style; built 1819–1824.

Old City Hall
Southwest corner of Fifth and Chestnut Sts.

Closed for restoration: check Visitor's Center, Independence National Historical Park, 116 South Third St. for opening.

United States Supreme Court shared these facilities with the City of Philadelphia from 1790 to 1800.

Merchants Exchange
Third, Walnut and Dock Sts.

Closed to public.

Fine example of Greek Revival style; erected 1832–34.

CONGRESS HALL
Sixth and Chestnut Sts. (southeast corner)

Hours: daily, 8:45–5. Admission free.

Rooms where United States House of Representatives and Senate met during 1790–1800.

CARPENTERS' HALL
320 Chestnut St.

Hours: daily, 10–4. Admission free.

Built for Carpenters' Company, 1770–1774. First Continental Congress met here, 1774.

Note: "New Hall" with Marine Corps museum on west side of Carpenters' Court; Pemberton House with Naval museum on east side of Court.

MAN-FULL-OF-TROUBLE TAVERN
129 Spruce St.   Tel.: (215) WA 2-1759

Hours: daily except Mon., 1:30–4:30; winter months, Sat., Sun. only, 1–4. Fee: adults, 50¢; children, 25¢.

Restored Tavern, built 1759.

CHRIST CHURCH

North Second St. (above Market St.)

Hours: daily, 9–5. Services: daily 12; Sun., 9, 11. Admission free.

Still an active parish, it is the oldest Anglican Church in the city. 15 signers of the Declaration of Independence worshipped here. Robert Morris and James Wilson are buried in churchyard. Built 1727–44; steeple added 1754.

PHILADELPHIA FIRE MUSEUM

149 North 2nd Street. Tel.: (215) MU 6-9700, Ext. 201

Hours: daily, except. Mon., 10–4. Admission free.

History of nation's oldest fire department; antique apparatus.

NEW MARKET AND HEAD HOUSE

Second and Pine Sts.

Built 1745–1800. Fire house at Pine St. built in 1805.

PERELMAN ANTIQUE TOY MUSEUM

268–70 South Second St.

Hours: weekdays, 9–5. Fee: adults, $1; children, 50¢.

Built circa 1760 for James Abercrombie, Philadelphia merchant.

FIRST BANK OF THE UNITED STATES

116 South Third St.

Hours: daily, 9–5. Admission free.

Building erected 1797. Later owned and operated as private bank by Stephen Girard. Now Visitor's Center for Independence National Historical Park.

POWELL HOUSE

244 South Third St. Tel.: (215) MA 7-0364

Hours: Tues.–Sun. 10–4. Fee: adults, $1; children, 12–16, 50¢; under 12, and Scouts, 25¢.

Colonial mansion and garden. Home of post-Revolutionary mayor of Philadelphia.

TODD HOUSE

Northwest corner Fourth and Walnut Sts.

Hours: Tel. 597-7018. Admission free.

1775 home of Dolley Payne Todd, later Mrs. James Madison.

BISHOP WHITE HOUSE
309 Walnut Street. Tel.: (215) 597-7018
Hours: write or telephone. Admission free.
Home of first bishop of Protestant Episcopal Church. Built 1786–87. Restored by National Park Service.

HILL-PHYSICK-KEITH HOUSE
321 South Fourth St. Tel.: (215) WA 5-7866
Hours: Tues.–Sat., 10–4; Sun., 1–4. Fee: adults, $1; children, 50¢.
Built in 1786; early 19th-century mansion and garden.

ARCH STREET FRIENDS' MEETINGHOUSE
Fourth and Arch Sts.
Hours: daily, 10–4; meetings for worship, Thurs., Sun., 10:30. Admission free.
Built 1804 on land given to Quakers in 1693 by William Penn. Philadelphia Yearly Meeting convenes here.

CHRIST CHURCH BURIAL GROUND
Fifth and Arch Sts. (southeast corner)
Hours: daily, 9–4. Admission free.
Benjamin and Deborah Franklin and five signers of the Declaration of Independence buried here.

FREE QUAKERS' MEETINGHOUSE
Fifth and Arch Sts. (southwest corner)
Hours: summers, daily except Mon., 10–5. Admission free.
Built 1783 by Free (Fighting) Quakers. Now headquarters of Junior League of Philadelphia.

BETSY ROSS HOUSE
239 Arch St.
Hours: daily, 9:30–5:15. Admission free.
Small Philadelphia mideighteenth-century house. Traditionally home of Betsy Ross.

UNITED STATES MINT
North Fifth St.
Hours: Mon.–Fri., 9–3:30. Admission free. Self-guided tours.
Glass-enclosed observation gallery allows view of entire coinage operation. Numismatic museum with special display.

PENN MUTUAL OBSERVATION DECK

Sixth and Walnut Sts. Tel.: (215) WA 5-7300

Hours: Apr. 1–Nov. 1; weekdays, 9–4; Sat., Sun., holidays, 10–6.

Splendid panoramic view of historic area and waterfront. Narrated description.

ATWATER KENT MUSEUM

15 South Seventh St.

Hours: daily, 9–5. Admission free.

Housed in old Franklin Institute building. Presents history of Philadelphia with dioramas, paintings, prints, models, and related objects.

ELFRETH'S ALLEY

Hours: daily, 1–4.

Alley is oldest continuously occupied residential street in the U.S. Several of the houses date from 1720's. Most houses open on Elfreth's Alley Day, the first Saturday in June.

Off Cherry Street, between Front and Second Sts.

ZOOLOGICAL GARDENS
34th St. and Girard Ave.

Hours: daily, 10–5. Fee: adults, $1; children, 2–11, 25¢; Children's Zoo, 25¢; Safari monorail: adults, 75¢; children, 50¢.

First zoo in the U.S. Over 2,000 animals, birds, reptiles. Animals may be fed, petted, in Children's Zoo. Safari monorail covers more than one mile of inner perimeter of zoo proper. Picnic facilities.

USS "OLYMPIA" (Admiral Dewey's Flagship)
Pier 11 north.

Hours: weekdays, 10–5; Sun. and holidays, 11–6. Fee: adults, $1; children, 50¢.

Dewey's flagship at Battle of Manila Bay, 1898. The ship closed her active service, in 1921, by bringing America's Unknown Soldier home from France.

At the foot of Race Street and Delaware Ave.

SECTION 8

New York City

This chapter includes outline information on some of the most famous places to visit, and more detail on others not so well known, in the five boroughs of the city. They are grouped in general areas so that several may be seen in a few hours. Driving is not recommended in lower and mid-Manhattan during the week; however, a few parking areas are suggested.

It may be helpful to remember that the avenues (and Broadway) run north or south while the streets run east or west. (With the exception of the main thoroughfares, which are two-way, even-numbered streets run east and odd-numbered streets run west.)

NEW YORK CONVENTION AND VISITORS' BUREAU
90 East 42nd St.   Tel.: (212) 687-1300

Call, write, or stop in for free maps, current event schedules, dining guides, tour brochures, tour suggestions for special groups, etc.

The following publications have current events listings: *Cue* magazine; *New York Magazine; New Yorker* magazine; *Parents Magazine* (Metropolitan Edition: lists of events of interest to families with children); *New York Times* newspaper.

Sightseeing bus tours can be the answer for those who prefer a conducted trip. The following offer a variety of tours, ranging from about 2 hours to 8 hours, that cover a small section to the entire city. Brochures and information can be obtained direct or from the Convention and Visitors' Bureau.

Crossroads Sightseeing Corp.
1572 Broadway (between 47th and 48th Sts.)   Tel.: (212) LT 1-2828

The Gray Line
900 Eighth Ave. (between 53rd and 54th Sts.)   Tel.: (212) 765-1600

Manhattan Sightseeing Bus Tours
150 W. 49th St.,   Tel.: (212) 255-6641

From N.J., if driving, it will be easiest to park on Rte. 3, just beyond Lincoln Tunnel exit from the N.J. Turnpike; well-marked lots with regular bus service to Port Authority Building, 8th Ave. and West 40th St. Other nearby parking areas: from Lincoln Tunnel, left or right ramp to Bus Terminal roof; or, north from Tunnel exit, then left on 41st or 42nd Sts. to West Side Airlines Terminal; other garages on 41st and 42nd St. or 10th Ave. From Bus Terminal, crosstown bus on 42nd St. For subway connections to all parts of city, consult Hagstrom's Map of Subways, available at stationery stores and some newsstands.

LOWER MANHATTAN

On weekends and holidays the area is virtually deserted and cars can maneuver easily. Another way to see the district is by renting a bicycle (the Visitors' Bureau will give you information).

From Lincoln or Holland Tunnel, and George Washington Bridge: West Side Highway to Battery Park. Large parking garage. Or, IRT Subway to South Ferry.

Statue of Liberty and Ferry Trip

Battery Park

Hours: daily, 9–4, on the hour. Fee: adults, 90¢; children, 5 to 11, 40¢.

Castle Clinton

Battery Park

In process of being restored, this National Monument was built as a fort to protect the harbor just prior to the War of 1812.

U.S. Customs House

Bowling Green

Erected on site of Fort Amsterdam. Contains the Rotunda Room with WPA murals of Reginald Marsh.

Fraunces Tavern

Pearl and Broad Sts.

Hours: weekdays, 10–4; closed Sat., Sun., holidays (except Washington's Birthday and Thanksgiving). Admission free.

Built as a private home in 1719, it became a popular tavern in 1762. Washington said farewell to his officers in the Long Room (1783). First floor restaurant.

Castle Clinton National Memorial. *National Park Service*

Trinity Church
Wall St.

Hours: open daily.

Founded in 1697; present building erected in 1846. Hamilton and Fulton among famous people buried in churchyard.

Federal Hall National Memorial. *National Park Service*

Federal Hall National Memorial
26 Wall St.

Hours: Mon.–Fri., 9–4:30. Admission free.

Site of Washington's inauguration as first President of the U.S. Museum of Colonial and early Federal periods of the city.

New York Stock Exchange
20 Broad St. (Exhibit Hall and visitors' gallery)

Hours: Mon.–Fri., 10–2:30.

Free guided tours of country's largest organized stocks and bonds market.

American Stock Exchange
86 Trinity Place

Hours: business days, 10–3.

Gallery overlooks Trading Floor. Multiscreen theatre; replica of Exchange in 1890's; audiovisual exhibits; multilingual guides.

Federal Reserve Bank of New York
33 Liberty St. Tel.: (212) RE 2-5700

Hours: Mon.–Fri. Tours: 1-hour; by appointment only: call Public Information, (212) RE 2-5700.

Depository for foreign countries' gold and for settling international accounts. Holds $13 billion worth of gold bricks. Worn-out currency destroyed here. Bank has excellent free map of Lower Manhattan.

City Hall
City Hall Park at Broadway and Fulton St.

Hours: Governor's Room, Mon.–Fri., 10–3.

Considered among the most beautiful buildings in America, this is a superb example of Federal period architecture. The Governor's Room has historic portraits and antique furniture including desks of the first three U.S. Presidents.

South Street Seaport Museum
16 Fulton Street Tel.: (212) 349-4310

Hours: daily (except Thanksgiving and Christmas), 12–6.

Center of the planned restoration of Fulton Fish Market area. Memorabilia, pictures, etc., of New York as a port city. Schooner, ships and tugs may be boarded.

Chase Manhattan Bank

1 Chase Manhattan Plaza   Tel.: (212) 552-6343

Hours: tours by appointment, weekdays, 9:30–3:30.

St. Paul's Chapel

Broadway and Fulton St.

Erected 1766. George Washington's pew, with the Great Seal of the U.S. above it, is preserved here.

Fire Department Museum

104 Duane St.

Hours: Mon.–Fri., 9–4; Sat., 9–1. Admission free.

Antique fire engines, equipment and exhibits of New York City firefighting.

Brooklyn Bridge

Opposite City Hall

First suspension bridge and still among the most beautiful. A walk across the bridge provides a splendid view of the Harbor.

Chinatown

West of Chatham Square

Interesting shops, good restaurants; Chinese Museum; Buddhist temple. For over a century the area has been the center of the city's large Chinese population.

Greenwich Village

West of Broadway from 14th St. south to about Spring Street.

Washington Arch

Washington Square

Designed by Sanford White in 1893.

Grace Church

Broadway and 10th St.

Great example of Gothic Revival architecture; designed by James Renwick when he was only 23. Famous stained glass windows.

Westbeth

Bethune St. at West St.

Ground area is display place for Westbeth's artists: pictures, photos, sculpture, all for sale. Remarkable old building with an elevated railroad spur track running through part of it.

East Village

East of 5th Ave., south of 14th St.

Many shops, boutiques, art and crafts boutiques.

African Tribal Art Gallery

84 E. 10th St. Tel.: (212) 982-4556

West African tribal art; masks, costumes, instruments used in everyday life and rituals. Clothing accessories for sale.

The Old Merchant's House

29 E. 4th St.

Hours: Tues.–Sun., for conducted tours, 2, 3, 4 P.M. Closed Mon., holidays, Aug. Fee: adults, 50¢; children under 12, 25¢.

Greek Revival house with furnishings, costumes of Seabury Tredwell family.

Cooper-Hewitt Museum of Decorative Arts & Design

3rd Ave. & 7th St.

Hours: Mon.–Sat., 10–5; closed Sat., June–Sept. Admission free.

A Smithsonian institution featuring textiles, drawings, wood and metal work, ceramics, furniture, etc.

St. Mark's-in-the-Bowery

2nd Ave. & 10th St.

Present structure erected in 1795 on site of Peter Stuyvesant's family chapel. He and many other prominent New Yorkers buried here.

Police Academy and Museum

235 E. 20th St.

Hours: Tours at 10 A.M. & 1 P.M., Mon.–Fri. Admission free.

Bil Baird Theatre

59 Barrow St. Tel.: (212) YU 9-7060

Hours: Sat., Sun., 1 and 3:30.

Bil Baird's marionettes in shows for children.

Walking Tour of Chelsea

First of self-guided walking tours of city's historic neighborhoods. Way marked by red, white and blue signs: start at old Siegel-Cooper Department store, 6th Ave. and 18th St.

Aerial view of New York looking north from about 23rd St. *New York Convention and Visitors Bureau*

Theodore Roosevelt Birthplace National Site
28 E. 20th St.

Hours: daily, 9–4:30. Fee: adults, 50¢; children under 16, free.
Birthplace and early home of the 26th President. Typical New York brownstone houses collection of Roosevelt's life and travels.

Flea Market
6th Ave. at 25th St.

Hours: Sundays only, spring and fall, weather permitting. Admission free.
Open-air attic with typical flea-market items.

MIDTOWN MANHATTAN
Parking is limited. Advise crosstown bus from Port Authority Bus Terminal.

EMPIRE STATE BUILDING AREA

St. Stephen's Church
147 East 28th St.

Gothic structure, notable for fine stained glass and supporting columns made from 19th-century ships' masts.

Empire State Building
34th St. and 5th Ave.

Hours: daily, 9:30–midnight. Fee: adults, $1.60; children under 15, 80¢.

Astro Gallery
155 East 34th St.

Hours: Mon.–Sat., 10–5. Admission free.
Interesting collection of semiprecious stones ranging from several tons to the very small. Minerals-gems library. Everything for sale.

Pierpont Morgan Library
29 East 36th St.   Tel.: (212) 685-0008

Hours: daily, except Sun., and holidays, 9:30–5; closed Sat., June–July; closed Aug. Admission free.
Tapestries, paintings, sculpture, rare books, documents, manuscripts, bindings, etc.

Celanese House
122 East 38th St.

Hours: Mon.–Sat., 9:30–5. Admission free.

Apartments decorated by five noted designers in this Georgian mansion with Flemish-bond brickwork.

GRAND CENTRAL AREA AND EAST
Grand Central Station
42nd St. and Lexington Ave.

Astroflash
Fee: $5.00

Give time and place of your birth and IBM computer, programmed by André Barbault, astrologer, gives you a horoscope. Machine can handle 3 languages.

United Nations Headquarters
46th St. and 1st Ave. Tel.: (212) 754-1234

Hours: tours begin every few minutes between 9:15 A.M. and 4:45 P.M. Fee: for tours, adults, $1.50; children under 12 and school groups, 50¢; children under 5 not permitted on tour. Admission to public areas free.

Tour shows operation of various world service agencies and the headquarters. Limited number of tickets, on first-come basis, to Security Council when in session. Check N.Y. newspapers for information of sessions.

TIMES SQUARE AND WEST
Hudson River Piers: check shipping news for liners in port; some may be seen before sailing; most charge small fee. Broadway and 42nd Street. Garment center. Theatre district nearby. Boat trip around Manhattan: Circle Line, Pier 83, West 43rd St. Tel.: (212) 563-3200. Tour about 3 hours.

Madison Square Garden Center
31st to 33rd Sts., between 7th and 8th Aves.

Hours: tours every hour on the half hour, Mon.–Sat., 9–5:30; Sun., 10–5:30. Fee: adults, $2.00; children, $1.00; students, $1.50.

Tour includes Center's seven facilities: the Garden, Felt Forum, Center Cinema, Bowling Center, Hall of Fame, and National Art Museum of Sports.

United Nations Secretariat Building. *New York Convention and Visitors Bureau*

MIDTOWN (Near 5th Ave., between 42nd and 59th Sts.)

Ford Foundation
320 E. 43rd St. Tel.: (212) 573-5000

Hours: tours Tues. at 3, Thurs. at 10 A.M. Admission free.

Indoor garden and pool area make a pleasant break.

New York Public Library and Bryant Park
5th Ave. and 42nd St. Tel.: (212) 790-6161

Hours: Mon.–Sat., 9 A.M.–10 P.M.; Sun., 1–10 P.M.

Changing program of exhibits throughout building. Children's Room famous for its historical collection of books, story-hour programs. During warm months, noontime concerts in Bryant Park, a tree-shaded oasis in midtown.

Eastman Kodak Gallery and Photo Information Center
1133 6th Ave. (at 43rd St.)

Hours: Mon.–Sat., 10–5:30. Admission free.

Photographic exhibits.

Union Carbide Building
Park Ave. and 47th St.

Hours: Mon.–Fri., 9:30–6; closed holidays. Admission free.

Changing national and international art exhibits.

Lever Brothers
390 Park Ave. Tel.: (212) 688-6000, Ext. 8038

Hours: Mon.–Fri., 10–5; weekends, holidays, 1–5. Admission free.

Building is the pioneer of stainless steel and glass design. Art exhibits in lobby: all media, varied and interesting exhibitions, primarily American artists' societies.

Rockefeller Center
49th to 51st Sts., west of 5th Ave.

Hours: tours, daily at frequent intervals, 9:30–5:30. Fee: adults, $1.90; children under 12 and students, $1.20.

Complex of 18 buildings around the sunken Plaza which is used for outdoor dining in summer and ice skating in winter. Changing floral displays in the Promenade.

Rockefeller Center Rink (Ice Skating)

Lower Plaza, 5th Ave. and 49th St.   Tel.: (212) 246-5810

Hours: daily during winter months, 10:30–12:30, 1–3, 3:30–5:30, 6–8, 8:30–10:30; weekends, 10:30–12, 1–2:30, 3:30–5, 6–8, 8:30–10:30. Fee: children under 12, $2.00, others, $2.50 on weekdays; weekends, $2.50 for all. Skate rental, $1.35.

Observation Roof

RCA Building

Hours: daily; April 1–Oct. 1, 10 A.M.–11 P.M.; Oct. 2–Mar. 31, 10–7. Fee: adults, $1.30; children under 12 and students, 80¢.

Excellent view of city.

NBC Radio and TV Studios

RCA Building

Hours: guided tours at frequent intervals from 9–7 daily. Fee: adults, $1.75; children under 14, 90¢.

Hour-long tour of radio and TV studios.

Chase Manhattan Bank Money Museum

1254 Sixth Ave. (near 50th St.)

Hours: Tues.–Fri., 10–5. Admission free.

Display of bank's collection of monies and articles used for money from 2500 B.C. to present.

Radio City Music Hall

50th St. and 6th Ave.

Hours: from 10:30. Fee: popular prices.

Feature film and Rockettes, Ballet Corps, symphony orchestra, organ music.

St. Patrick's Cathedral

5th Ave. and 50th St.

Hours: daily, 6 A.M.–8:30 P.M.

Gothic design inspired by Cathedral of Cologne.

Museum of Famous People

133 W. 50th St.   Tel.: (212) 586-2616

Hours: opens Mon.–Sat. 10 A.M.; Sun., opens noon. Fee: adults, $1.50; children under 12, 90¢.

Wax museum.

Delacorte Geyser and Sutton Place
One block east of Antiques Center at the East River.
The fountain can be seen from a small waterfront park; it is in the river at the tip of Welfare Island. Sutton Place, north of the park, up to 59th St., has lovely old town houses.

Museum of Modern Art
11 W. 53rd St.
Hours: Mon.–Sat., 11–6; Thurs., 11–9; Sun., 12–6. Fee: adults, $1.50; children under 16, 75¢; group rates.
Modern painting, sculpture, drawings, prints, architecture, industrial and graphic design. Old and modern films (not on commercial circuit) shown daily, 2 and 5:30; occasional films at 8 P.M. Check magazines and newspapers for listings.

Museum of Contemporary Crafts
29 W. 53rd St.
Hours: weekdays, 11–6; Sun., 1–2. Fee: adults, 75¢; children under 12, 25¢.
Imaginative displays of American crafts and skills.

Museum of American Folk Art
49 W. 53rd St.   Tel.: (212) LT 1-2474
Hours: Tues.–Sun., 10:30–5:30. Fee: adults, 25¢; students, 15¢; children under 12, free.
Changing exhibits of native art: figureheads, cigar store Indians, trade signs, etc.

Museum of Primitive Art
15 W. 54th St.
Hours: Tues.–Sat., 12–5; Sun., 1–5. Fee: adults, 50¢; students, 25¢.
Exhibits of ancient and contemporary primitive cultures.

"The Mill"
Burlington House, 1345 6th Ave. (at 54th St.)   Tel.: (212) 333-5000
Tours: Tues.–Sat., 10–7. Admission free.
Moving walkway past machines that spin, wind, knit, board, weave, buft and dye. Ride takes 8½ minutes and is accompanied by flashing lights, music, mirrors and color photos.

Owens-Corning Glass
717 5th Ave. (at 56th St.)
Hours: Mon.–Sat., 9:30–5. Admission free.
Exhibits of products made with Corning glass and fiberglas.

IBM Gallery of Arts and Science
16 E. 57th St.
Hours: Mon.–Sat., 10–5. Admission free.
Exhibits of art, photographs, design and science.

General Motors
767 5th Ave.
Hours: Mon.–Fri., 9–9; Sat., 11–7. Admission free.
Exhibit demonstrates scope of GM's national and internationl manufacturing. Automobiles, product displays, research and engineering exhibits.

New York Cultural Center
2 Columbus Circle   Tel.: (212) 581-2311
Hours: Tues.–Sun., 11–8. Fee: adults, $1.00; children under 12, 50¢.
Changing exhibits of American and international painting, sculpture, graphics, etc. Building designed by Edward D. Stone.

New York Coliseum
Columbus Circle
Largest exposition center in country. Many shows open to public: check newspapers.

UPTOWN MANHATTAN
CENTRAL PARK AREA (59th St. to 110th St.)
For east side of Park, take Madison Ave. bus (north) or 5th Ave. bus (south); for west side, take 8th Ave. (IND) Subway.

Central Park
Famous Central Park Zoo with nearby pony rides. Children's Zoo; Delacorte Theater; 2 skating rinks; model yacht pond; carousel; 2 rowing lakes; horseback riding; outdoor festivals and theatre: check newspapers for special events. Hansom cab rides start at Plaza, 5th Ave. and 59th St.

Bethesda Fountain, Central Park. *New York Convention and Visitors Bureau*

The Bible House
Broadway at 61st St.
Hours: Mon.–Fri., 9–4:30. Admission free.
Rare editions of the Scriptures in more than 1,000 languages. Copies of 1st edition of King James Bible. Write for reservations for group tours.

Asia House
112 E. 64th St.
Hours: Mon.–Fri., 10–5; Sat. 11–5; Sun., 1–5. Admission free.
Old and contemporary examples of Japanese art.

Temple Emanu-El
5th Ave. and 65th St.
Hours: daily, 10–5. Admission free.
Oldest Reform synagogue in city.

175

Frick Collection

1 East 70th St. (just off 5th Ave.)

Hours: Tues.–Sat., 10–6; Sun., holidays, 1–6; June–Aug. 31: Sun, Wed., holidays, 1–6; Thurs., Fri., Sat., 10–6. Closed major holidays. Admission free; no children under 10.

A great city mansion with European masterpieces from 14th to 19th centuries.

Lincoln Center for the Performing Arts

Broadway and 64th St.

Hours: guided tours, daily at frequent intervals, 10–4. Fee: adults, $1.85; students, $1.25; children under 12, $1.00.

Year-round center for music, drama, dance.

Lincoln Center of the Performing Arts. *New York Convention and Visitors Bureau*

Whitney Museum of American Art

Madison Ave. at 75th St.   Tel.: (212) 249-4100

Hours: Mon.–Sat., 11–6; Tues., 11–10; Sun., 12–6. Fee: adults, $1.00; children under 12, free with adult.

Changing exhibits of American art: painting, line drawings, watercolors, sculpture, etc. Film library showings: daily, 12, 2, 4; Tues. also at 6, 8. Admission included in entry price.

New-York Historical Society
170 Central Park West, at 77th St.

Hours: Tues.–Fri., and Sun., 1–5; Sat., 10–5. Closed holidays, August. Admission free.

Extensive collections of period furniture, prints, paintings, sculpture, old fire engines, carriages. Museum and library focus on American history, especially that of New York City.

American Museum of Natural History
Central Park West at 79th St.

Hours: Mon.–Sat., 10–5; Sun., holidays, 1–5; closed Thanksgiving, Christmas. Fee: donation.

Halls of the Dinosaur, American Indian, Ocean Life, Biology of Fishes, Man in Africa, Earth History, Biology of Invertebrates. Animals in their natural habitat. Recorded tours through portable tape recorders may be rented: in English, Spanish, French, German.

Hayden Planetarium
Central Park West at 81st St.   Tel.: (212) 873-1300

Hours: Mon.–Fri., 2, 3:30; Sat., 11, 1, 2, 3, 4, 5; Sun., 1, 2, 3, 4, 5. Fee: adults, $1.50; children under 16, 75¢.

Zeiss VI projector reproduces movements of stars and planets. Program changes 6 times a year.

Metropolitan Museum of Art
5th Ave. and 82nd St.

Hours: Mon.–Sat., 10–5; Sun., holidays, 1–5; Tuesdays until 10. Fee: donation required.

One of the world's great museums. Collections range from ancient days to present. American Wing has entire rooms from early American homes. Many visiting collections. Check newspaper or *Cue, New York, New Yorker, Parents Magazine* for current exhibits. Portable tape recorded tours for rent.

Guggenheim Museum
5th Ave. at 89th St.

Hours: Wed.–Sat., 10–6; Tues., 10–9; Sun., holidays, 12–6; closed July 4, Christmas and Mon. except when Mon. is a holiday. Fee: 50¢; children under 6, free; student groups, 25¢.

Notable building designed by Frank Lloyd Wright. Modern paintings, graphics, sculpture in changing exhibits.

National Academy of Design
1083 5th Ave.

Hours: daily, 1–5. Admission free.

Exhibit center for display of interior designs: furniture, fabrics, wall and floor coverings, china, glassware, etc.

Jewish Museum
5th Ave. and 89th St.

Hours: Mon.–Thurs., 12–5; Fri., 11–3; Sun., 11–6. Fee: adults, 50¢; children under 12, 25¢.

Mansion houses ceremonial objects, paintings, relics from Jewish history. Contemporary painting, sculpture.

Museum of the City of New York
5th Ave. and 104th St.   Tel.: (212) 534-1672

Hours: Tues.–Sat., 10–5; Sun., holidays, 1–5. Admission free.

Exhibits illustrate New York City's history from days of Dutch settlers to present: costumes, theatrical memorabilia, photos, prints, etc.

HARLEM AREA (110th St. to 155th St., from Morningside, St. Nicholas and Colonial Parks east to 5th Ave. and Harlem River.)

There are many famous churches in the area, notably the Abyssinian Baptist Church. The Saint Nicholas Historic District is on 138th and 139th Sts. between 7th and 8th Ave. Fine examples of architecture by McKim, Mead, and White are on 139th Street. For bus tour of the area:

Penny Sightseeing Co.
303 W. 42nd St., N.Y., N.Y. 10036   Tel.: (212) 247-2860

Fee: vary with type of tour; group rates.

Tours range from 3 to 4½ hours. Stops include Harlem Hospital, Harlem Branch of N.Y. Public Library housing famous Schomburg Collection, Apollo Theatre, Freedom Bank, Abyssinian Baptist Church, etc.

Studio Museum in Harlem
5th Ave. at 125th St.

Hours: Mon., Wed., 10–9; Thurs., Fri., 10–6; Sat., Sun., 1–6. Admission free.

Changing exhibits of contemporary Black artists.

WEST SIDE, NORTH OF CENTRAL PARK

Cathedral of St. John the Divine (Episcopal)
Amsterdam Ave. and 112th St.

Hours: daily, 7–6.

Built of stone in Gothic style. Now about ¾ complete.

Riverside Church (Interdenominational)
Riverside Drive and 122nd St.

Lovely tower of the Gothic structure contains the 74-bell Laura Spelman Rockefeller Carillon.

Riverside Museum
310 Riverside Drive

Hours: Tues.–Sun., 2–5. Fee: adults, 75¢; children under 12, 35¢.

Permanent collection of Nepalese and Tibetan art.

General Grant National Memorial
Riverside Drive and 122nd St.

Hours: daily, 9–5. Admission free.

Burial place of our 18th President and his wife. Battle flags, etc.

WASHINGTON HEIGHTS AREA (Broadway and 155th St.)

Chapel of the Intercession
Hours: weekdays, 6:30–6; Sun., 7:30–6.

Old bell, cast in 1704, rings the Angelus. Audubon's Grave and monument.

Museum of the American Indian, Heye Foundation
Hours: Tues.–Sun., 1–5; closed legal holidays and Aug. Admission free.

World's largest collection of Indian art and culture from North, Central and South America.

Hispanic Society of America
Hours: Tues.–Sat., 10–4:30; Sun., 2–5. Admission free.

Fine examples of Spanish and Portuguese art and culture. Many masterpieces of Spanish art.

American Numismatic Society
Hours: Tues.–Sat., 10–5; Sun., 1–4. Admission free.
Large collection of coins from ancient days to present; medals.

American Geographical Society
Hours: Mon.–Fri., 9–4:45. Admission free.
Interesting collection of historic maps.

JUMEL MANSION
161st Street and Edgecombe Ave.
Hours: Tues.–Sun., 11–4:45. Admission free.
Erected in 1765, this Georgian-style house was Washington's headquarters during the retreat from New York in 1776. Now a museum of the Revolutionary period.

DYCKMAN HOUSE
Broadway and 204th St.
Hours: Tues.–Sun., 11–5. Admission free.
Dutch farmhouse, now museum of the colonial period.

THE CLOISTERS
Fort Tryon Park, near Fort Washington Ave. and 191st St.
Hours: Tues.–Sat., 10–5; Sun., 1–5 (to 6 P.M. during summer). Fee: donation.
Building incorporates parts of several medieval monasteries and chapels from Europe; excellent collection of art of medieval period. Picnic area; snack bar.

THE BRONX
From West Side Highway (Henry Hudson Parkway) to Cross Bronx Expressway, watch for Bronx Park exit signs.

Bronx Park

Bronx Park (New York Zoological Park)
Hours: daily, 10–5. Fee: Fri.–Mon., adults, 75¢; children 6–12, 50¢. Tues.–Thurs., admission free.
One of largest collections of birds, reptiles and mammals in country. World of Darkness for nocturnal animals; and African Plains animals separated from public by a moat.
Southwestern portion of the park.

New York Botanical Garden

Hours: daily, 10–sunset. Greenhouses open daily, 10–4. Admission free.

Flowers, shrubs and trees from all parts of the world. Museum and library.

In northwestern section of park: follow signs.

Poe Cottage

Kingsbridge Road and Grand Concourse

Hours: Tues.–Sat., 10–1 and 2–5; Sun., 1–5; closes 4 P.M. during winter. Admission free.

Where Poe lived from 1846 to 1849 while writing many of his most famous works.

From Fordham Road, left on Grand Concourse.

Van Cortlandt Mansion

Broadway and 242nd St.

Hours: Mon., 12–5; Tues.–Sat., 10–5; Sun., 2–5. Fee: Sun.–Wed., 25¢ other days free.

House restored, furnished and maintained by the Colonial Dames of America. Built 1748. Fine examples of 17th- and 18th-century colonial Dutch furnishings.

In Van Cortlandt Park.

Dutch bed in Van Cortlandt Mansion

181

BROOKLYN

Brooklyn Heights Historic District
Adjacent to downtown Brooklyn

Overlooking East River, with superb view of Manhattan skyline, this is a 50-block area of 19th-century New York architecture at its best. Good walking tour. Many boutiques, restaurants.

From Brooklyn or Manhattan Bridges, right on Tillary Street, then left on Court Street, right on any of side streets. Or, Lexington Ave. IRT Subway to Court Street or Seventh Ave. IRT Subway to Clark St. (St. George Hotel).

The following are centrally located near Prospect Park and Eastern Parkway. Take Seventh Ave. IRT Subway to Prospect Park-Brooklyn Museum station. From West Side Highway, south through Brooklyn Battery Tunnel; Queens Expressway to Prospect Expressway to Prospect Park exit.

Brooklyn Museum
188 Eastern Parkway

Hours: Mon.–Sat., 10–5; Sun., holidays, 1–5; closed Christmas. Admission free.

Arts of the Americas; famous collections of primitive, Oriental and Egyptian art; European masters. Outdoor sculpture garden. Fine museum shop.

Brooklyn Botanic Garden
1000 Washington Ave.

Hours: daily 10 A.M.–sunset. Admission free.

Famous Japanese Garden; mass plantings of flowering cherry trees; fragrance garden for the blind.

Adjoins Prospect Park.

CONEY ISLAND
Most facilities closed winter months.

Amusement park, beach, skating rink, restaurants.

From Goethals Bridge to Staten Island Expressway; across Verrazano Narrows Bridge then left onto Shore Parkway (Belt System) to Coney Island exit.

New York Aquarium

8th St. and Surf Ave., Coney Island

Hours: daily; Labor Day–May 31, 10–5; June 1–Labor Day, 10–9. Fee: adults, $1.00; children 5–16, 50¢.

Large and varied collection of rare and beautiful fish and marine life, including whales, seals, penguins.

Beluga whale making his bird-like squeak asking for supper. Aquarium at Coney Island. *New York Convention and Visitors Bureau*

QUEENS

John F. Kennedy International Airport

Idlewild, Queens

Hours: all day. Fees for Control Tower, observation deck.

Shore Parkway to exit.

The following may be reached from the Queens Expressway to the Long Island Expressway; or, from Queens Midtown Tunnel in Manhattan to Long Island Expressway.

Bowne House
38–01 Bowne Street
Hours: Tues., Sat., Sun., 2:30–4:30. Admission free.
House built by John Bowne in 1661. He was the Quaker who led the fight for religious freedom in Dutch colonial times. **Northern Blvd.: Bowne St. is between Main St. and Parsons Blvd.**

Flushing Meadows-Corona Park
Flushing
Facilities include marina, boating, carousel, indoor ice skating, picnicking, swimming pool, N.Y. State Pavilion, Queens Arena.

Queens Zoo and Children's Farm Zoo
Hours: 10–4, daily. Admision free.

Queens Botanical Garden
43–50 Main St. (part of park)
Hours: daily, 9–dusk.

Hall of Science of the City of New York
Hours: Tues.–Sat., 10–5; Sun., 1–5. Admission free.
Space Park contains full-sized space vehicles. Exhibits of space exploration, atomic energy, communications systems.

Shea Stadium
Home of New York Mets and Jets.

STATEN ISLAND
Easily reached from N.J. via Goethals Bridge, Outerbridge Crossing, or Bayonne Bridge.

Staten Island Ferry Ride
From St. George, Staten Island to Battery Park, Manhattan. Passengers, round trip, 10¢. Boats leave every few minutes. Views of New York skyline, Governor's Island, Statue of Liberty, Lighthouse.

Staten Island Institute of Arts and Sciences
Stuyvesant Place and Wall St., St. George
Hours: Tues.–Sat., 10–5; Sun., 2–5; July, Aug., Tues.–Sat., 10–4. Admission free.
Displays of natural history, fine arts, dioramas of Indians.

One block west of ferry entrance in St. George.

Clove Lakes Park
1150 Clove Rd., West Brighton
Facilities include excellent bridle path, boating, fishing, ice skating rink, model yacht pond, picnicking.

Staten Island Zoo
Broadway and Clove Rd., West Brighton
Hours: daily, 10–5. Admission free.
Small but outstanding zoo with one of country's largest reptile collections.

Across street from Clove Lakes Park, in Barrett Park.

Richmondtown Restoration
Richmond Rd., Richmond
Former county seat of Staten Island, village was founded in late 17th century. Restoration now in progress.

Voorlezer's House
Built in 1695, the oldest standing elementary school in the county.

Staten Island Historical Society Museum
Hours: Tues.–Sat., 2–5; Sun., 2–6. Admission free.
Excellent collection of early American tools, implements.

Third County Courthouse
In Greek Revival style, the courthouse was built in 1837.

St. Andrew's
This Episcopal school was founded in 1708. Present building, in Victorian Gothic style, was built in 1872.

Conference House
Foot of Hylan Blvd., Tottenville

Hours: Tues.–Sat., 10–5 (closes 4 P.M. Oct.–Apr.); closed Mon. except when a holiday. Fee: Tues., Thurs., free; other days, adults, 25¢; children under 12, free when accompanied by adult.

Built in 1668. Here Lord Howe met with members of the Continental Congress in the only peace conference of the Revolutionary War.

Jacques Mardrais Center of Tibetan Art
340 Lighthouse Ave., Richmondtown

Hours: Apr.–Oct., Tues.–Fri., 2–5; also 2nd and 4th Sat. and Sun. of each month. Fee: 50¢.

Collection of Tibetan art and manuscripts; Tibetan Temple; sculpture in terrace gardens. Not recommended for youngsters.

INDEX

Abraham and Warren Vreeland House, 27
Absecon Hall (Atlantic City), 133
Absecon Lighthouse, 134
Abyssinian Baptist Church, 178
Academy of Natural Sciences, 153
Acorn Hall, 16
Adventure Hill Farm, 60
African Tribal Art Gallery, 166
Airports: John F. Kennedy International, 183; Newark, 46; Teterboro, 29
Aline Wolcott Museum, 113
Allaire State Park and the Deserted Village of Allaire, 105
Allen House, 102
ALPINE, 31; Boat Basin, 31
American Geographical Society, 180
American Indian: Cape May County Historical Museum, 150; Hunter-Lawrence House, 127; Monmouth County Historical Association, 99; Morris Museum of Arts and Sciences, 9; Museum of the American Indian, Heye Foundation, 179; N.J. State Museum, 84; Red Barn Museum, 141; Salem County Historical Society, 144; Schoolhouse Museum, 43; Space Farms Early American Museum, 5; Staten Island Institute of Arts and Sciences, 185; Sussex County Historical Society, 6; Zabriskie (Von Steuben) House, 42
American Museum of Natural History, 177
American Numismatic Society, 180
American Stock Exchange, 164
American Wax Museum, 154
Amusement parks, playlands: Asbury Park, 106; Belmar, 106; Bertrand Island, 7; Bowcraft's Sport Shop and Playland, 67; Bradley Beach, 106; Coney Island, 182; Fairy Tale Forest, 10; Gingerbread Castle, 9; Manasquan, 106; Million Dollar Pier, 133; Seaside Heights, 121; Steel Pier, 133; Steeplechase Pier, 133
Anheuser-Busch Brewery, 47
Animal farms: Adventure Hill Farm, 60; Centerville & Southwestern Railroad on the Becker Farm, 21; College Farm (Rutgers), 93; DeCous Certified Farm Market and Hilltop Orchards, 143; Hopatcong Bear Farm and Zoo, 7; Pocono Wild Animal Farm, 56; Queens Children's Farm Zoo, 184; Space Farms, 5; State Fish Hatchery, 57; State Game Farm (pheasant), 120; State Pheasant Farm, 57
Ann Whithall House, 128
Anthony Wayne Recreation Area, N.Y., 34
Apollo Theatre, 178
Appalachian Trail, 10
Arch Street Friends' Meetinghouse, 158
ARCOLA, 40
Arrowhead Ski Area, 99
Art exhibits, galleries: African Tribal Art Gallery, 166; Eastman Kodak Gallery, 171; Foundation of the Arts and Sciences, 122; Highgate Gallery, 27; IBM Gallery of Arts and Sciences, 174; Lever Brothers, 171; Newark Public Library, 45; Pierpont Morgan Library, 168; Princeton University Art Museum, 88; Rutgers University Art Gallery, 94; Studio Museum in Harlem, 178; Union Carbide Building, 171; Wesbeth, 165
ASBURY PARK, 106
Ashbrook Golf Course and Reservation, 66
Asia House, 175
Astroflash, 169
Astro Gallery, 168
ATLANTIC CITY, 133, 134; Marina, 134

195